HILLSIDE HOME PLANS

HILLSIDE HOME PLANS

Selected by the editors of
Hudson Home Guide

BANTAM/HUDSON BOOKS
New York, New York • Los Altos, California

HILLSIDE HOME PLANS

A Bantam Book/published in association with
Hudson Home Publications, February 1979

Executive Editor, Robert J. Dunn; Book Editor, Jane Hess;
Project Editor, Sandra L. Beggs; Art Director, Annette T. Yatovitz;
Cover Rendering, Kenneth Vendley; Production Manager, Laurie
Blackman; Plans Manager, Elayne Pappis; Plans Assistants,
Sandy Rollings, Nancy Gillett.

Cover plan appears on page 101

ISBN 0-553-M01172-3

Published simultaneously in the United States and Canada

Bantam Books are published by Bantam Books, Inc. Its
trademark, consisting of the words "Bantam Books" and the
portrayal of a bantam, is registered in the United States Patent
Office and in other countries. Marca Registrada. Bantam Books,
Inc., 666 Fifth Avenue, New York, New York 10019.

Printed in the United States of America
Library of Congress catalog card number 79-50294

ABOUT THIS BOOK

Building your home from a pre-designed plan can be one of the most satisfying projects you've ever undertaken, as hundreds of people discover every year. The 76 homes presented in this Bantam/Hudson book were developed by architects, designers and commercial plan services who take full advantage of the latest construction techniques and newest building materials. The plans in this book offer you a wide range of diversified architectural styles and floor plans to fit your family's tastes and needs. Minor changes in specifications may be necessary, and many of the plans offer alternate interior design options for that reason. The plans selected for this book are all designed to suit less-than-level lots. If your building site has a terrific view that you want to take advantage of, or the lot has a side slope, then one of these homes could be just what you're looking for. Often, through the use of a daylight basement, the plan achieves additional living space that enhances the overall living conditions. Flexible site options are offered with many of the plans to accommodate your particular lot. We hope that one of these plans will provide you with the home you've always wanted.

Photography: Steve Marley

Building Your Home from a PRE-DESIGNED PLAN

For each of us who dreams of building our own home or entrusting a custom job to a contractor of our selection, the first step towards reality is the selection of a well-defined set of plans. No lender will grant construction funds, no city or local government will issue a building permit, and certainly no contractor will pick up a hammer in our behalf without being given blueprints describing exactly what we want built.

WHERE TO GET BLUEPRINTS

Many homeowners-to-be resolve this situation by employing the full services of a local architect or building designer who can transfer ideas, thoughts, likes, dislikes and pretty magazine pictures to lines that establish construction activities. On the other hand, far more homeowners-to-be rely on the services provided by architects, designers and plan service firms who specialize in creating pre-designed plans sold at modest prices. This group of experts can trace their efforts to literally hundreds of thousands of homes built across the United States.

SELECTING A SITE

Most housing experts suggest that you secure a home site before making the complete decision on house style, size and features. This is sound advice, but many homeowners through careful search and selection have first found the plans for their dream home and then purchased the necessary lot. Either way, the lot must suit the plans and the plans must fit the lot.

In buying land, it is wise to obtain the advice of a local realtor, appraiser or lending official before signing on the dotted line. These persons deal in such transactions on a daily basis and can help you to avoid hidden pitfalls. There is nothing more frustrating than to buy a site and then find for one reason or another that you can't build upon it, or that it has various restrictions preventing you from constructing the home that you have always dreamed about.

Be aware of the deed restrictions that may prevent construction of a two-story home, if this is what you wish, or restrictions that demand a two-story model when your heart is set on a rambling ranch. Likewise, check your local building department for set-back and side-yard clearance, where you may or may not build a garage, what easements may exist for roadways or public utilities, whether sewers are required or a septic tank may be used, etc.

WHAT IS A PRE-DESIGNED PLAN?

Pre-designed plans presented in this and other home plan books available from Bantam/Hudson are basically simplified versions of the working drawings which may be purchased and are much easier to read than detailed blueprints. Designers of stock plans often expect you to make a few minor changes in their designs to customize the plan for your specific needs. In fact, they sometimes anticipate these changes by offering a number of design options. For example, a plan may come with two alternate interior layouts, changing the same square footage to different use. Other plans may be designed with or without a basement and, depending upon your needs and locale, you can specify which alternative is best for you. Occasionally, you'll find a plan that you like but the orientation is wrong for your site — many plan companies will offer mirror or full reverse plans for a modest additional cost. If the plan you select doesn't offer all the options you need, it's sometimes a simple matter for a builder to make the necessary changes before construction. Or you may wish to contact a local architect or designer who can bring about the changes you deem necessary. Local professional help often is well worth the extra few dollars involved, and can serve as a safeguard against costly errors when plans are being changed.

If you want to make major changes in a pre-designed plan, order only one set of plans. Some building codes will allow minor changes to be made on your working drawings without being completely redrawn; other codes may require redrawing by an architect or plan service before they allow any changes. After the plans have been modified, you'll need four to eight complete sets of plans for local building departments,

continued

lending institutions, subcontractor cost estimators, and actual construction.

Although there are differences from company to company, generally most plan packages include a basement and foundation plan, floor plans for each level, exterior elevations, elevations of interior items, such as cabinetry and fireplaces, and cutaway sections and details of framing and special features. The package usually includes a list of "quality types" for the basic construction materials (grades of lumber, etc.), but not always a quantity list because changes are often made prior to or during construction. Some plan packages include electrical diagrams but omit plumbing and heating/cooling layouts since requirements for these vary across the country.

SELECTING A PRE-DESIGNED PLAN

Selecting a pre-designed home plan is much like being fitted for a fine, tailored suit. The end product must be attractive, provide the styling you desire and be comfortable to the user. You and your family are the prime considerations in the selection of a successful house plan. You must clearly understand your needs and best meet them with a design that accommodates your way of living as well as your current and long-range earnings.

Pre-designed plans, such as those featured in this Bantam/Hudson book, are intended for building sites with average characteristics rather than unique ones. However, most plans can usually be adapted to specific needs with regard to the lay of the land. This, of course, isn't true if you want to put a hillside home on a flat parcel of land.

If you have the benefit of having your land already purchased, make every effort to get to know it better before selecting a home plan. Visit the site at different times of the day and walk the property, visualizing how you and your family will make use of it — both from inside and outside the house. Note the site orientation to the sun as well as auto traffic. Take into account the presence of young and mature trees that will later provide shade and aesthetic beauty to the dwelling. Relate the site to your outdoor living needs.

Imagination and visualization are imperative in planning a new home. Your pre-designed house plans will be two-dimensional, but you must think three-dimensional space. Picture yourself living in the plan under consideration. Mentally walk through the entry door and behold what will appear. Are you smack in the middle of the living room which merely serves as a hallway to get to other rooms? If so, look for another plan. Privacy is a major factor in enjoyable living. Your home should be "zoned" for the way you will most enjoy it:

- The public area with its living room, dining room, entry, powder room
- The service area with kitchen, laundry, mud room or family lavatory, family room
- The private area including bedrooms and master bathroom

Select a house plan with the needed rooms and square footage, making certain that the circulation pattern or foot traffic doesn't crisscross areas needlessly. Walking from one end of the house to the other to use a bathroom is inconvenient as well as carpet-wearing. And traffic that passes through the kitchen work triangle is just a plain nuisance. Choosing the right plan for you and your family won't be easy, but the hours spent now will only be moments compared to later years of enjoyment. Get the entire family in on the act and compile a notebook with chapters on each room, detailing overall interior styling and exterior appearance.

Pre-designed plans are commonly accepted by the construction industry nationwide and have been the blueprint to efficient, enjoyable, economical contemporary homebuilding for many satisfied American families. Hopefully this book will provide you with a plan that will fit your needs and lifestyle in that long-awaited dream home.

How important are specifications?

Very. Specifications are an essential part of the total plans package which spell out in detail exactly how your home is to be constructed and with what materials. You or your architect must specify every desired feature, including manufacturer and model number or a brief description. A good contractor will help, but ultimately this is your responsibility. Remember that your contractor can be held legally responsible for only the materials described in the specifications, and if entries are vague or omitted, you'll probably end up paying extra.

14. LATH AND PLASTER:

Lath ☐ walls, ☐ ceilings: Material.................................... ; weight or thickness ....
Dry-wall ☑ walls, ☑ ceilings: Material *sheetrock* ; thickness *½*
Tape and finish as recommended by manufac

15. DECORATING: *(Paint, wallpaper, etc.)*

ROOMS	WALL FINISH MATERIAL AND APPLICATION
Kitchen	*Pinehill paneling - Georgia-Pacific*
Bath	*2 coats flat oil*
Family room	*Rio Grande paneling - Georgia-Pacific*
all other	*sheetrock and 2 coats latex*

16. INTERIOR DOORS AND TRIM:

Doors: Type *Flush* ; material ....
Door trim: Type *Moulded* ; material *Fir* Base: ....
Finish: Doors *2 coats varnish* ; trim: ....
Other trim *(item, type and location)* *all trim will have 2 c*

Personalizing a Pre-designed Plan

A recent survey by the editors of Hudson Home publications has indicated that nine out of ten persons who purchase a pre-designed plan and actually build, modify the plan considerably before construction. More often than not, the modifications involve some degree of structural alterations from the basic plan and, when they do, we strongly recommend the layman use professional assistance to insure sound structural planning, economy where possible and that the aesthetics of the plan remain intact. The sample below is an actual modification. The owners extended the depth of the home by a few feet and added and expanded on the exterior deck situations, front and back. However, the key to the modifications, the personalization factor, can be seen in the many interior changes and additions the owners prescribed to make their plan a suitable one for their lifestyle.

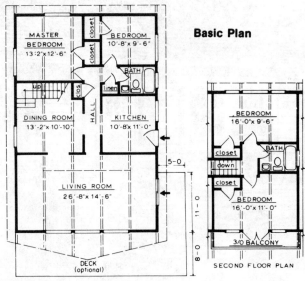

Basic Plan

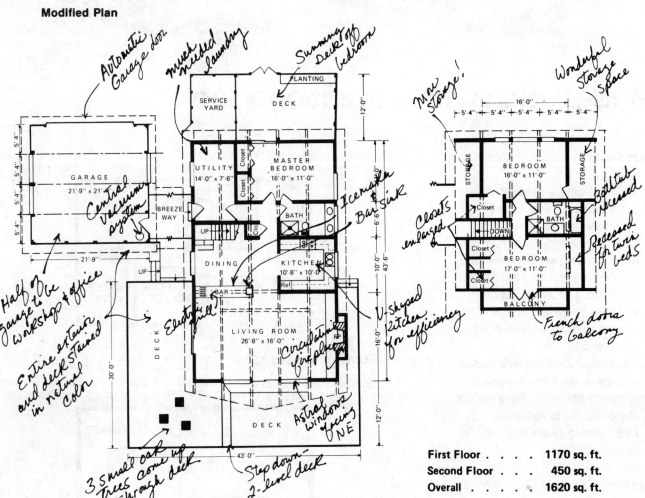

Modified Plan

First Floor	. . .	1170 sq. ft.
Second Floor	. . .	450 sq. ft.
Overall	. . . . .	1620 sq. ft.

Modest plan with a traditional look

PLAN 2263

- Colonial detailing enhances the exterior of this three-bedroom home
- L-shaped living room has formal dining area conveniently located adjacent to the kitchen
- Compact L-shaped kitchen includes breakfast area and has access to rear patio for outdoor entertaining
- Basement level houses washer and dryer and extra storage space to the rear of the garage
- Materials list is included
- Full reverse plans cost an additional $30

Designer: National Plan Service

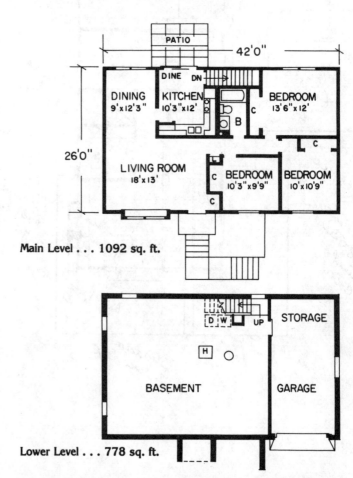

Main Level . . . 1092 sq. ft.

Lower Level . . . 778 sq. ft.

Design is adaptable to a variety of activities

PLAN 5105

- Entryway is at half level in this home, designed for a hillside
- Two bedrooms are located on the upper level, each with its own private bath and skylight
- Dining room, living room and spacious kitchen complete the upper floor
- Woodburning fireplace in living room has built-in bookcases on both sides
- Accessible from the dining room is a large wood deck for easy meals outdoors
- Lower level has three additional bedrooms, recreation room, workshop/storage room and a third bath
- Mirror reverse plans cost an additional $5

Designer: Jerry Gropp, AIA

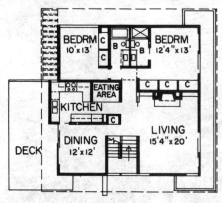

Upper Level . . . 1325 sq. ft.

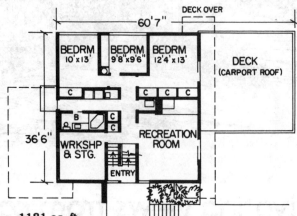

Lower Level . . . 1181 sq. ft.

11

Captivating views from continuous deck

PLAN 4213

- Attractive hillside plan takes advantages of a good rear view
- Three sets of sliding glass doors lead to spacious deck on main level
- Lower level has three bedrooms, each with sliding glass door access to the back yard
- Bonus loft room above dining area has private corner deck
- Large fireplace adds intimate touch to spacious living room
- Serving bar between kitchen and dining room eases mealtimes
- Mirror reverse plans available if specified

Designer: Claude Miquelle Associates

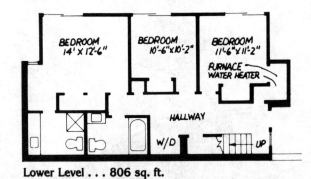

Lower Level . . . 806 sq. ft.

Main Level . . . 880 sq. ft.

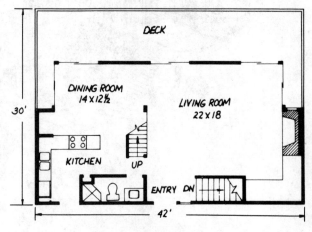

Upper floor is devoted to master bedroom suite

PLAN 6206

- Tiled entryway in this beautiful home design leads to two bedrooms on the right side of the ground level and to activity areas on the left
- For maximum privacy, the entire second level is devoted to a master bedroom suite, complete with compartmentalized bath
- Bathroom includes large tub and dual lavanity with access to a secluded sun balcony
- Basement level contains two additional bedrooms with bath and a family room with fireplace
- Mirror reverse plans costs an additional $10

Designer: Plans West

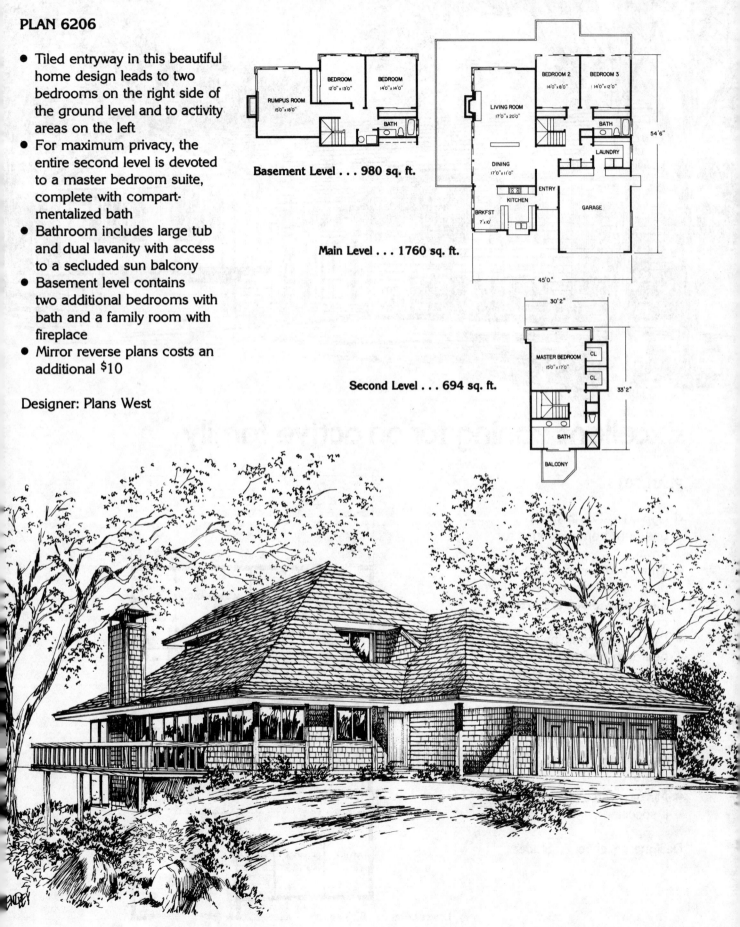

Basement Level . . . 980 sq. ft.

Main Level . . . 1760 sq. ft.

Second Level . . . 694 sq. ft.

Excellent zoning for an active family

PLAN 6013

- Upper level of this four-bedroom home is zoned for privacy
- Three bedrooms occupy the right side of the home while the activity areas are located on the left
- Lower level contains a fourth bedroom perfect for guests, a family room, study and bath, as well as a separate laundry room
- Dining room on upper floor is adjacent to L-shaped kitchen and has a view of the patio area through sliding glass doors
- Mirror reverse plans available if specified

Designer: Michael A. Studer

Upper Level . . . 1395 sq. ft.

Lower Level . . . 823 sq. ft.

Total coordination of interior and exterior

PLAN 2264

- Four-bedroom plan has lots of space for activities
- Large living room has sliding glass doors leading to front balcony
- Dining area is adjacent to galley-style kitchen and also has sliding glass doors leading to rear patio
- Master bedroom has private dressing area and shares bath with two other bedrooms on this upper level
- Laundry room, second bath and storage space complete the lower level
- Materials list is included
- Full reverse plans cost an additional $30

Designer: National Plan Service

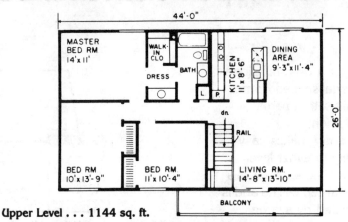

Upper Level . . . 1144 sq. ft.

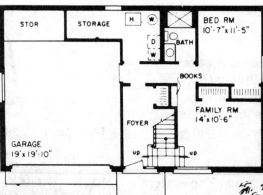

Lower Level . . . 675 sq. ft.

Polygonal-shaped home for down-sloped lot

PLAN 2519

- Designed for a downhill slope, this polygonal-shaped home can be built with a partial or full basement
- Split level entry makes easy accessability to either level
- Living-dining-kitchen area has a sloped beamed ceiling and is visually divided by a large central fireplace
- Three sliding glass doors and a deck extend the full length of the house
- Angled end bedroom walls extend beyond the front portion of house to provide a view
- Lower level has its own fireplace in the spacious game room

Designer: Robert Martin Englebrecht

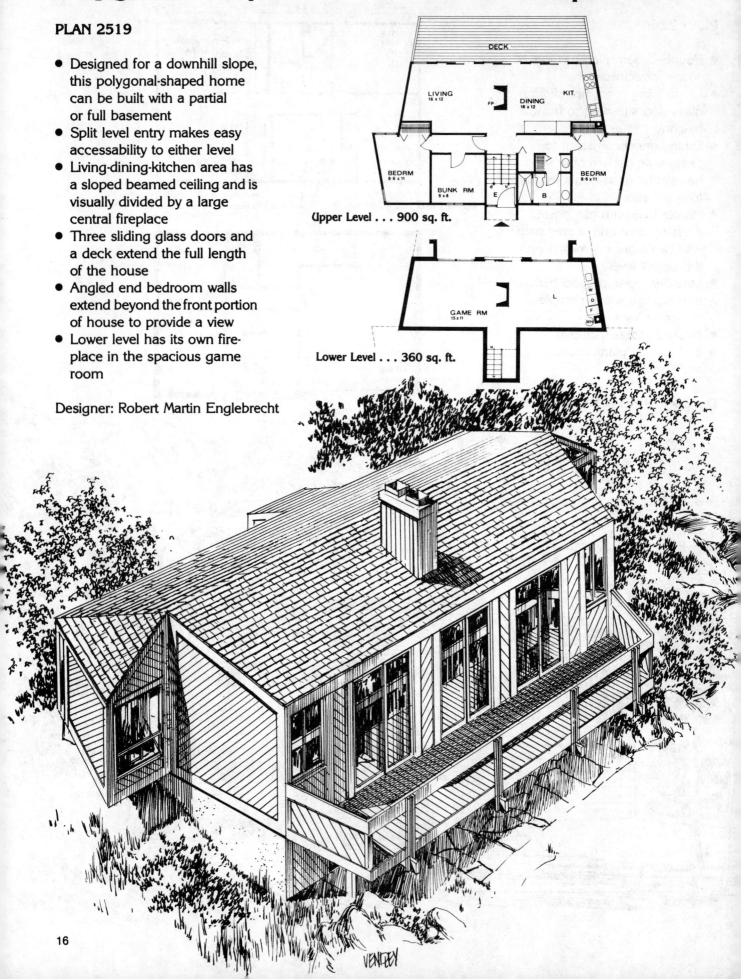

Upper Level . . . 900 sq. ft.

Lower Level . . . 360 sq. ft.

Staggered rooflines create eye-catching exterior

PLAN 7203

- Large flagstone entry sets tone for three-bedroom contemporary
- Open floor plan allows free movement to all areas of home
- Secluded for privacy, den has built-in bookshelves
- Storage area is adjacent to balcony loft that overlooks living room
- Child's playroom and extra storage accessible from garage
- Alternate second floor plan provides sauna and luxurious bathroom as extension of master bedroom
- Sweeping deck off living areas; small private deck off master suite
- Materials list is an extra $20
- Mirror reverse plans are an additional $15

Designer: Spectrum-3

Second Floor . . . 1284 sq. ft.

Alternate Second Floor Plan
(replaces child's playroom)

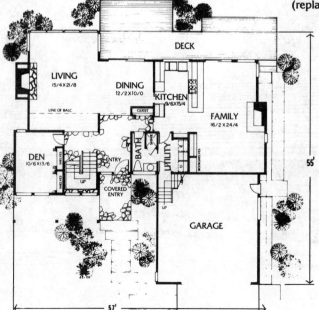

First Floor . . . 1542 sq. ft.

17

Stone and wood combination provides feeling of warmth

PLAN 4346

- A combination of wood and stone accent the exterior of this plan
- Well-designed interior separates sleeping quarters from activity areas
- Large activity room with vaulted ceiling has central fireplace with windows on either side to take advantage of a view
- Kitchen features a U-shaped work area and pass-through
- Two bedrooms and bath on main floor; one bedroom and bath on lower floor with connecting sun deck
- Materials list costs $10
- Mirror reverse plans available if specified

Designer: W. D. Farmer

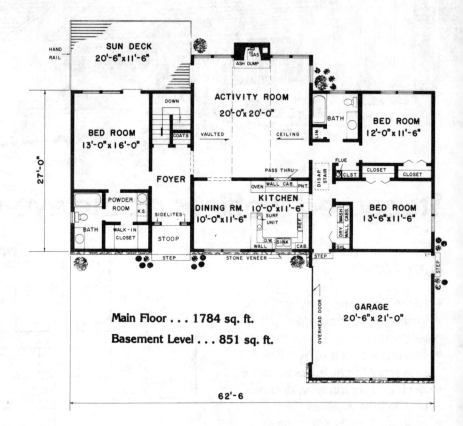

Main Floor . . . 1784 sq. ft.
Basement Level . . . 851 sq. ft.

Home for the growing family

PLAN 3801

- Three bedrooms plus spare room in daylight basement for use as additional bedroom, guest room or study
- Spacious recreation room is located on lower level
- Kitchen conveniently located between breakfast nook and dining room
- Adjacent redwood deck makes outdoor meals a pleasure
- Attractive entry separates bedrooms from active living and dining areas
- Three-and-one-half baths
- Materials list costs $20
- Full reverse plans cost an additional $20

Designer: Home Building Plan Service, Inc.

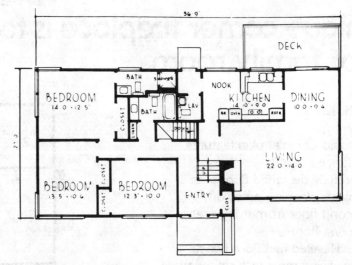

Main Floor . . . 1472 sq. ft.

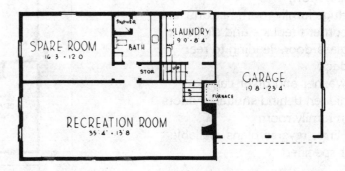

Basement

Unique corner fireplace is focal point of family room

PLAN 4215

- Classic Colonial plan features balanced styling
- Carefully designed floor plan isolates sleeping areas on second floor from living areas on first floor
- Multi-leveled first floor boasts large living room with cathedral ceiling, adjacent dining room, U-shaped kitchen with break-fast room
- Huge family room has unusual corner fireplace and sliding glass doors leading to rear deck
- Washer and dryer can be hidden behind shuttered doors in family room
- Mirror reverse plans available if specified

Designer: Claude Miquelle Associates

Second Floor . . . 840 sq. ft.

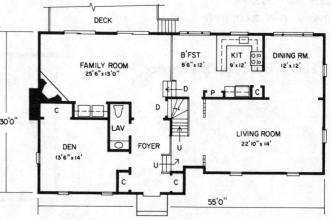

First Floor . . . 1538 sq. ft.

Decks abound for outdoor living enjoyment

PLAN 2747

- Dramatic modern styling for the contemporary family
- Multi-level floor plan makes the most of living space
- Cooking, eating and working areas are located on the lower levels
- Three bedrooms, two baths and living room occupy upper levels
- Living room has bar with sink and sunken conversation pit with fireplace for cozy get togethers
- Each bedroom has its own private sun deck
- Materials list is included
- Mirror reverse plans available if specified

Designer: Henry D. Norris, AIA

Upper Level . . . 1591 sq. ft.

Lower Level . . . 602 sq. ft.

Ranch-style home zoned for privacy

PLAN 4345

- Spacious ranch-style home designed for a hillside site
- All bedrooms are secluded in one side of home
- Master bedroom suite has dressing room, private bath, walk-in closet and access to sun deck through sliding glass doors
- Family room also connects with deck and features built-in fireplace with gas jet
- Large kitchen has adjacent breakfast room with bow window and utility room
- Plan also includes separate dining room for formal meals
- Materials list costs $10
- Mirror reverse plans available if specified

Designer: W. D. Farmer

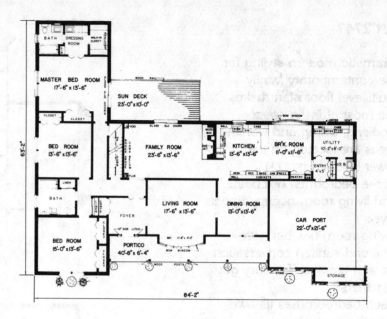

Living Area . . . 2744 sq. ft.

BASEMENT

Contemporary design is carried through to interior

PLAN 7207

- Four distinct levels of spacious floor area
- Contemporary exterior is carried through to interior
- Entry and living/dining area have vaulted ceilings
- Exterior is cedar siding with generous wood trim at all corners and critical areas
- Lower level features large recreation room, fourth bedroom and den/study
- Two decks off upper level living room expand space
- Three bedrooms and two baths occupy entire third level
- Materials list costs $20
- Mirror reverse plans cost an additional $15

Designer: Spectrum-3

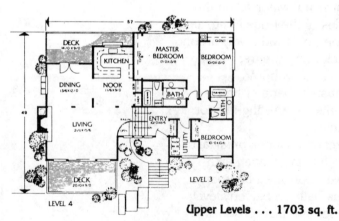

Upper Levels . . . 1703 sq. ft.

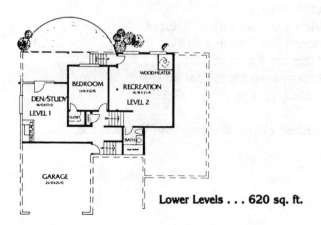

Lower Levels . . . 620 sq. ft.

Pentagonal plan with the outdoors in mind

PLAN 3802
PLAN 3802-A (without basement)

- Cathedral windows on three sides of the huge living/dining room, plus wide wrap-around deck bring the trees inside this second home
- Unusual shape of house creates interesting interior angles
- Kitchen includes breakfast bar adjoining open area
- Two good-sized bedrooms plus bath on balcony level;
- Basement plan provides additional recreation and utility space
- Plan available with or without basement. Please specify
- Materials list costs $20
- Full reverse plans cost an additional $20

Designer: Home Building Plan Service, Inc.

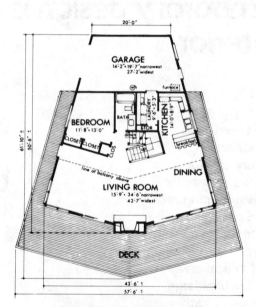

First Floor . . . 1108 sq. ft.

Second Floor . . . 625 sq. ft.

Lots of space for entertaining, indoors and out

PLAN 2152

- Pleasing blend of stone and wood accent exterior of this plan
- Designed for a sloping site favoring a rear view
- Two rear decks provide lots of space for outdoor entertaining
- Kitchen features indoor barbecue, breakfast bar and pass through to outer deck
- Living room has cathedral ceiling and built-in fireplace
- Large recreation room on lower level offers plenty of space for social gatherings with bar and fireplace
- Materials list costs $15
- Mirror reverse plans available if specified

Designer: Ron Dick

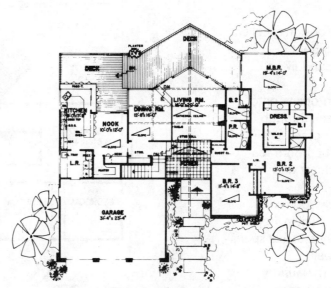

Main Level . . . 2422 sq. ft.

Lower Level . . . 1266 sq. ft.

Compact home fits snugly on side-sloping lot

PLAN 6014

- Contemporary design excellent for a side-sloping lot
- Split levels expand living areas
- Roomy kitchen opens onto angled rear deck through sliding glass doors
- Large master bedroom features walk-in closet and separate bath
- Spacious family room on lower level has built-in fireplace with extended hearth that spans full length of wall
- Fourth bedroom, laundry room and powder room complete the lower level
- Mirror reverse plans available if specified

Designer: Michael A. Studer

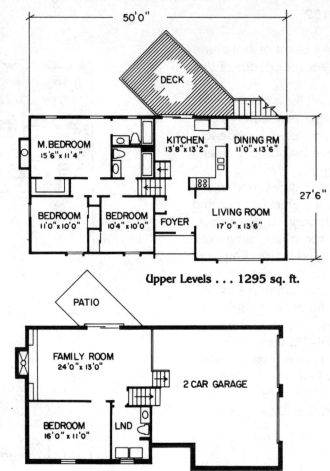

Upper Levels . . . 1295 sq. ft.

Lower Level . . . 633 sq. ft.

Designed for a sharply sloping site

PLAN 5004

- Tri-level plan takes advantage of steep, difficult site
- Street entry leads down flight of stairs to main living area
- Glass wall of living/dining room opens to rear deck
- Kitchen features pass-through to breakfast nook with adjacent deck
- Family room, two more bedrooms and second bath are on ground level, with another long deck
- Bonus studio with balcony on third level is a quiet retreat
- Mirror reverse plans available if specified

Designer: Habitec/Mike O'Hearn

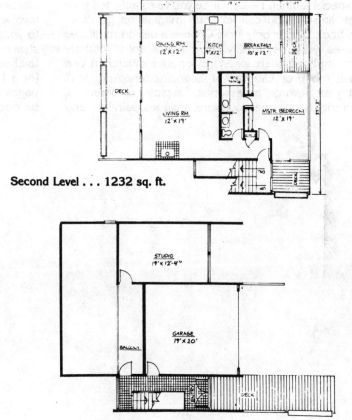

First Level . . . 771 sq. ft.

Second Level . . . 1232 sq. ft.

Third Level . . . 565 sq. ft.

Workable Kitchens

What is a workable kitchen? Just about anything you want it to be. Workable doesn't mean just utilitarian or functional, workable means a kitchen designed just for you and your family — aesthetically as well as functionally. The importance of the kitchen in the home should never be underestimated, nor should the appearance and design. Let's face it, you spend a lot of time there so why not make it an enjoyable as well as efficient place to be? First, think in terms of your own lifestyle and personality as it relates to the kitchen. Does your family tend to gather there? Are you prone to good old-fashioned sit-down meals, or is mealtime just a grab-and-run affair? If you entertain a lot or fancy yourself the gourmet cook you'll have special kitchen needs. Once you've established your kitchen lifestyle you can let your imagination go. Your pocketbook is your only limit. Choose a design motif that expresses your personality. How about some country charm, or ultra-modern, or an indoor-outdoor kitchen, or a Spanish motif, or Oriental, or Scandinavian. And don't forget your favorite accessories. Displays of ceramics, copper molds, gourmet cookware, antiques, paintings and other objects can help reflect the mood you desire. Color is another very important factor in the overall appearance of your kitchen. The color you choose for your appliances plays a major role in your decorating scheme. If bold appliance colors are selected, for example, they automatically become a dominant factor in the color scheming of your kitchen. The bolder the color, the more they begin to function as a focal point and cannot be ignored when planning your color surround. Where the kitchen adjoins the family room or is openly related to another area, keep the flow of color constant. Don't use one color here and another there. The effect is too jarring. Instead, achieve a variety with tints and shades of color. Decorating your kitchen can be a lot of fun, but it also involves many important decisions. Pay special attention to your selection of a wallcovering, floorcovering, cabinet style and their storage capabilities, and lighting. You'll want to choose these carefully since they're going to be around for a long time. The kitchens you'll see on the next few pages are good examples of how all these elements can be combined to result in pleasing, workable spaces.

Country charm abounds in this kitchen filled with historic mementos. The owners of this home like the warmth and homey feeling that lots of wood, brick, tile and braided rugs can give to a kitchen. By starting with any of the basic-shaped kitchens available you can create the kind of feeling you want if you pay careful attention to details and the building materials you use.

Photographer: Jim Brett

EFFICIENT KITCHEN WITH SPANISH FLAVOR

Earnest cooks like their work space beautifully equipped and inviting. The kitchen shown here is full of practical and pleasing ideas, and the flavor is subtly Spanish. Center stage is a butcherblock island, a definite step-saver that serves a multitude of purposes. This island lets you cook on it, chop on it and serve from it. Handpainted ceramic tiles inlaid in stucco rim the range hood and provide a Spanish motif to the kitchen. Matching tiles on the walls enhance the theme. A second built-in range also has an indoor barbecue for grilling. Kitchen has walls of storage cabinets — a must for the gourmet cook.

Photographer: Jim Brett

INNOVATIVE KITCHEN LOOKS
FRESH AS A DAISY

A lot of imagination went into the design of this kitchen. The kitchen is long, so the space is divided into three areas. The main working area is at one end where the range, ovens and countertop cutting space are located. The central part of the kitchen includes the sink and dishwasher plus additional cutting space. And the third area is devoted to space for informal meals with a built-in table that protrudes from the wall out into the main kitchen space. Floral wallpaper gives a fresh, crisp look.

CLEAN, SLEEK AND MODERN

Below Left: Dark and cluttered kitchens are more and more becoming a thing of the past. Today's homeowner wants an open, airy kitchen that allows visual contact with other areas of the home. The kitchen shown here has two such areas. Counter on right separates the kitchen working space from the family room, allowing the cook to take part in family functions, and the sliding glass doors at one end provide access to outdoor activities on the rear deck.

COMPACT KITCHEN FOR THE MINI-CHEF

Below Right: If cooking is not your forte you probably want a smaller kitchen that is an efficient, no-nonsense time-saver. This kitchen packs a lot of work space into a small area. In a few steps you can reach the ovens, refrigerator, dishwasher, sink, range and countertop/cutting board — an absolute study in efficiency. Soffit lighting spotlights the work areas, and floor is easy-care tile. Photo: Hager Manufacturing Company.

Photo: Riviera Cabinets

Photographer: Jim Brett

A KITCHEN WITH SPARKLE

Above Left: You don't have to spend a fortune to create a beautiful kitchen. A good choice of wallpaper combined with imaginative accessories will perk up your work area without spending your life savings. The mylar wallpaper selected for the kitchen above transforms what could have been a drab kitchen into a room with a sparkling character. Wall-length shelves provide space for your cherished accessories. Wallpaper is from James Seeman Studios, Inc.

PRACTICAL AND PRETTY ISLAND KITCHEN

Above Right: Kitchen islands come in many different sizes and shapes, but they all have one thing in common — they're a big help to the harried householder. Basically, an island is planned to simplify kitchen functions, and such is the case with the island illustrated above. Ample drawer and cabinet space is located in the base of the unit. The top has space for mixing, chopping, cooking and meal planning. Copper range hood has additional storage above and seemingly floats in mid air.

Take advantage of the rear view

PLAN 3914
PLAN 3914-A (without basement)

- Designed to take advantage of rear view of sloping lot
- Vaulted ceilings over living room and all three bedrooms
- Spacious deck spans rear of home and adjoins both living and dining rooms
- Master bedroom on second floor has walk-in closet and private deck
- Laundry room conveniently located near U-shaped kitchen
- Covered walk leads to entry
- Fireplace is located at end of large, open living/dining area
- Plan available with or without basement. Please specify
- Materials list costs $20
- Full reverse plans cost an additional $20

Designer: Home Building Plan Service, Inc.

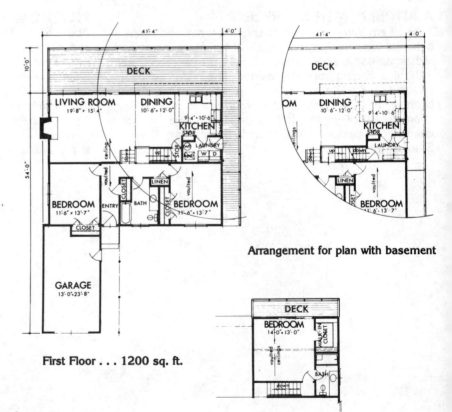

First Floor . . . 1200 sq. ft.

Arrangement for plan with basement

Second Floor . . . 360 sq. ft.

Octagonal plan for an all-round view

PLAN 3897
PLAN 3897-A (without basement)

- Exciting octagonal design provides 360 degrees of view
- Central fireplace provides a focus point for the living room and a source of additional heat
- Large enough to serve as a year-round home as well as a vacation home
- Encircling deck maximizes both view and living areas
- Plan available with or without basement. Please specify
- Materials list costs $20
- Full reverse plans cost an additional $20

Designer: Home Building Plan Service, Inc.

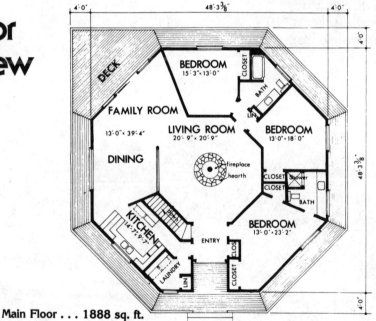

Main Floor . . . 1888 sq. ft.

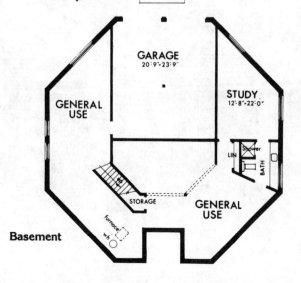

Basement

Plan takes advantage of a rear view

PLAN 3222

- Perfect plan for a site with a rear view
- Nestled on lower floor are two bedrooms, bath, utility room and sunken activity room with fireplace
- Breakfast nook and dining room on main floor have sliding glass doors leading to large rear deck
- Glass wall in sunken living room makes most of the view
- Luxurious master bedroom suite on upper floor boasts corner fireplace, sun deck, circular tub, walk-in wardrobe and adjacent study
- Materials list costs $10
- Mirror reverse plans available if specified

Designer: L. M. Bruinier

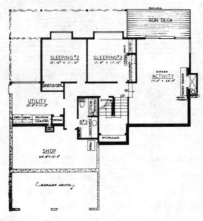

Basement . . . 1852 sq. ft.

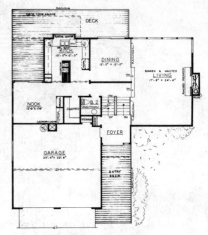

First Floor . . . 1235 sq. ft.

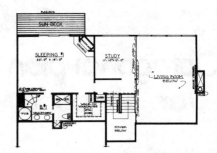

Second Floor . . . 892 sq. ft.

Rear View

Glassed-in greenhouse for gardening enthusiasts

PLAN 7208

- Bold, innovative plan has dramatic open spaces
- Garden entry court bids visitors welcome
- Glassed-in greenhouse overlooks spacious rear deck
- Kitchen features eating bar
- Two-story living room has fireplace with stone hearth
- Master bedroom suite on main floor includes private sun deck
- Upper floor boasts two large bedrooms with full bath
- Large recreation room with den, shop and utility room conveniently located on basement level
- Materials list costs $20
- Mirror reverse plans cost an additional $15

Designer: Spectrum-3

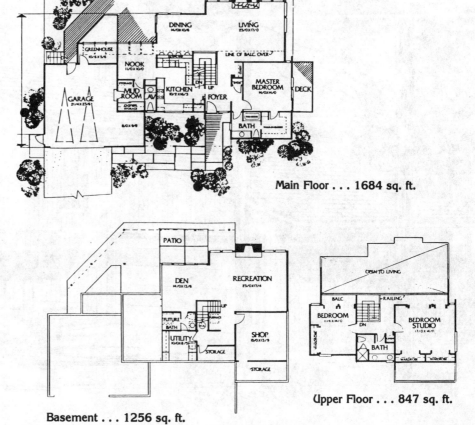

Main Floor . . . 1684 sq. ft.

Basement . . . 1256 sq. ft.

Upper Floor . . . 847 sq. ft.

37

Contemporary year-round or holiday home

PLAN 3952
PLAN 3952-A (without basement)

- Compact plan has three bedrooms and three baths
- Large living room with fireplace has glass wall to take advantage of view
- Efficient U-shaped kitchen is adjacent to dining area and laundry room
- Second floor has railing overlooking living room below
- Spacious deck provides outdoor living area
- Plan available with or without basement Please specify
- Materials list costs $20
- Full reverse plans cost an additional $20

Designer: Home Building Plan Service, Inc.

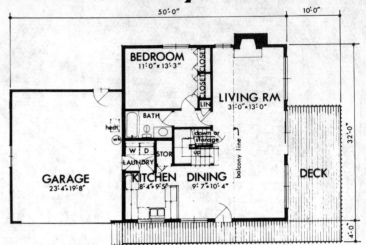

Compact split-level offers living flexibility

PLAN 3838
PLAN 3838-A (please specify)

- Attractive compact design with choice of two interior layouts to suit your needs
- Plan 3838 has L-shaped kitchen with separate dining room. Plan 3838-A has U-shaped kitchen adjacent to family room
- Both plans include daylight basement, with recreation room, bath and extra bedroom or den
- Living room is enhanced by picture window view, vaulted ceiling and fireplace
- Materials list costs $20
- Full reverse plans cost an additional $20

Designer: Home Building Plan Service, Inc.

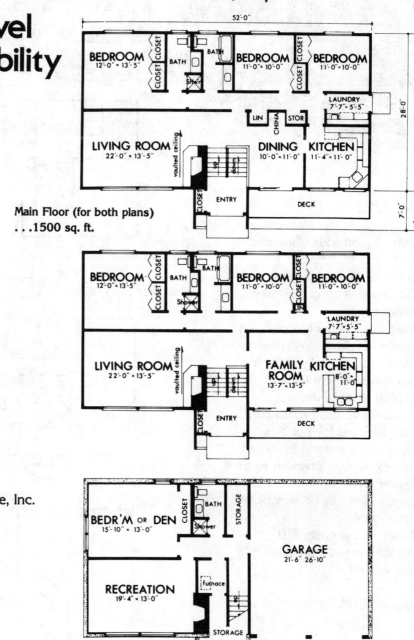

Main Floor (for both plans)
...1500 sq. ft.

Basement ... 884 sq. ft.

Spacious plan has Southern Colonial accents

PLAN 3223

- Classic plan with columned portico is reminiscent of Southern Colonial style
- Gracious winding staircase enhances foyer
- Main level offers lots of living space with large living room, family room, study and wide open kitchen containing central work island
- Good-sized utility room can also be used for hobbies
- Upper level master bedroom has extra-large dressing room
- Lower level can be used for family activities or as separate apartment
- Materials list costs $10
- Mirror reverse plans available if specified

Designer: L. M. Bruinier

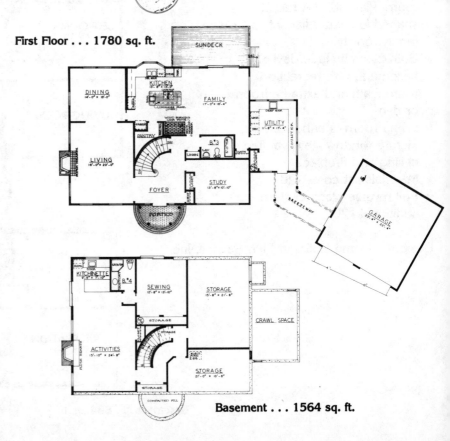

Second Floor . . . 1564 sq. ft.

First Floor . . . 1780 sq. ft.

Basement . . . 1564 sq. ft.

Home that fits easily on 50-foot lot

PLAN 2062

- Split-level design that can fit a narrow 50-foot lot
- Living and dining room are a 29-foot open area
- Efficient kitchen includes breakfast space, storage pantry
- Balcony-type stairway leads to three bedrooms, all with big closets, and a possible two baths
- Large recreation room with bay window offers many uses
- Materials list is included
- Mirror reverse plans available if specified

Designer: Master Plan Service

Living and Bedroom Levels . . . 1232 sq. ft.

Entrance Level . . . 451 sq. ft.

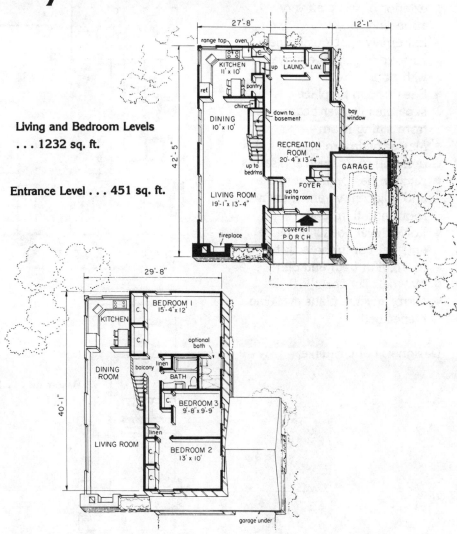

Luxurious living with a Spanish flair

PLAN 3225

- Spanish accents make the exterior of this plan very appealing
- Extremely spacious home surrounds central courtyard with pool
- See-through fireplace separates master bedroom from sitting room
- Master bedroom also includes dressing room, bath and sauna
- Kitchen has breakfast nook and adjacent veranda, utility room and third bath
- Lower level boasts fireplace and wet bar in the activity room, fifth bath and den
- Materials list costs $10
- Mirror reverse plans available if specified

Designer: L. M. Bruinier

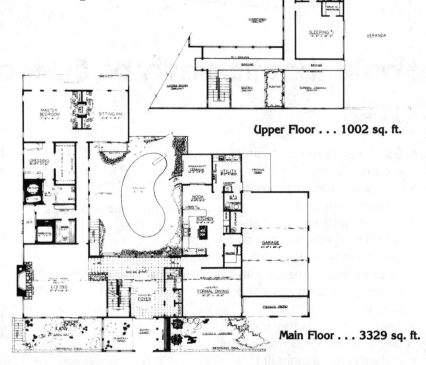

Upper Floor . . . 1002 sq. ft.

Main Floor . . . 3329 sq. ft.

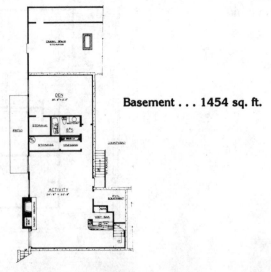

Basement . . . 1454 sq. ft.

Lower level garage adds to home's attractiveness

PLAN 3622

- Rustic split-level plan designed for gently sloping lot
- Raised entrance level is same as living room, dining room and kitchen, with bedroom wing higher
- Front living room is enhanced by bay window and endwall fireplace
- L-shaped kitchen affords space for dinette table
- Terrace off dining room is ideal for outdoor meals
- Laundry and storage are behind garage, as well as utility area
- Materials list is included
- Full reverse plans available if specified

Designer: Garlinghouse

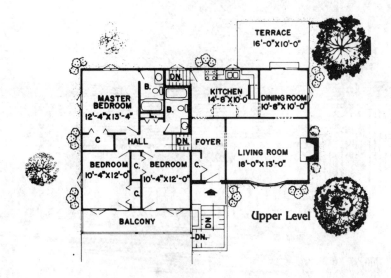

Upper Level

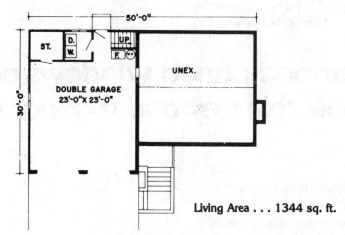

Living Area . . . 1344 sq. ft.

Diamond-paned windows and stone chimney add exterior interest

PLAN 3328

- Massive stone fireplace dominates sunken family/living room with cathedral ceiling
- Three ample bedrooms are sequestered in separate wing away from activity areas
- Wet bar in dining room is convenient to adjoining wood deck for outdoor entertaining
- Roomy breakfast area off galley kitchen has closeted space for laundry equipment
- Please specify foundation option: slab, crawlspace or basement
- Materials list costs $10
- Mirror reverse plans available if specified

Designer: W. L. Corley

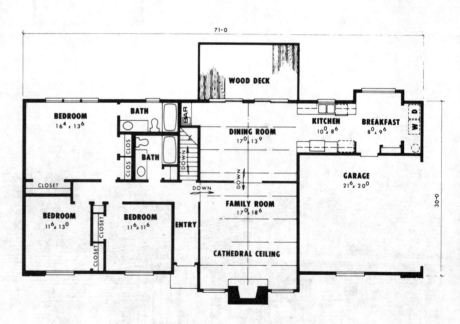

Living Area . . . 1740 sq. ft.

Designed for sites with a view

PLAN 3862

- Two-level plan takes advantage of the view
- Dining and living rooms have sloped ceilings and expansive view through picture windows
- Sliding glass doors provide access to spacious raised deck
- Upstairs bedroom/study has balcony rail overlooking the dining and living areas below
- Plan has two full baths, separate laundry room, and convenient storage space behind garage
- Materials list costs $20
- Full reverse plans cost an additional $20

Designer: Home Building Plan Service, Inc.

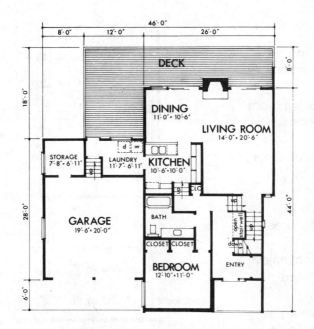

First Floor . . . 1117 sq. ft.

Second Floor . . . 674 sq. ft.

Pillars express charm and welcome guests

PLAN 3630

- Stately white pillars add Colonial charm to comfortable design
- Plan boasts sizable living room with fireplace and separate dining room
- Bedroom wing includes three bedrooms, one with built-in shelves
- Centrally located bath with double sink serves all three bedrooms
- Lower floor family room enjoys full bath with shower and access to rear patio
- Materials list is included
- Full reverse plans available if specified

Designer: Garlinghouse

PATIO

BEDROOM
12'-0" X 12'-4"

B.

C.

KITCHEN
10'-0" X 12'-4"

DINING ROOM
9'-8" X 12'-8"

SHELVES

C.

HALL

C.

LIVING ROOM
19'-4" X 14'-8"

BEDROOM
10'-0" X 11'-0"

BEDROOM
9'-0" X 11'-0"

C.

PORCH

First Floor . . . 1200 sq. ft.

Basement . . . 1176 sq. ft.

PATIO
22'-8" X 10'-0"

B.

D.
W.

GARAGE
19'-4" X 26'-8"

FAMILY ROOM
17'-8" X 26'-8"

28'-0"

FURN.
H.W.
S.

DRIVE

PORCH

42'-0"

A variation of the standard A-frame

PLAN 7504

- Vacation home is a variation of the standard A-frame design
- 25'x25' square floor plan has prow-shaped two-story glass expanse facing wrap-around wood deck for full advantage of a view
- Dramatic wood beam cathedral ceiling, rugged stone wall corner fireplace with dome-shaped hood, plank flooring and sliding glass doors to deck enhance living room
- Spiral staircase takes you up to two bedrooms on the second floor
- Materials list is included
- Mirror reverse plans available if specified

Designer: National Home Planning Service

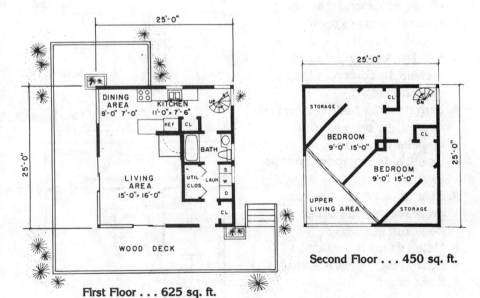

First Floor . . . 625 sq. ft.

Second Floor . . . 450 sq. ft.

Dramatic rooflines complement modern design

PLAN 2746

- Spacious entry with large coat closet is a winter-weather plus
- Great room with fireplace allows an expandable dining room for those special occasions
- Efficient kitchen includes breakfast nook and window greenhouse
- Large master bedroom on first floor offers privacy from upstairs bedrooms
- Optional family room on lower level
- Rear deck accessible from great room and master bedroom
- Materials list is included
- Mirror reverse plans available if specified

Designer: Henry D. Norris, AIA

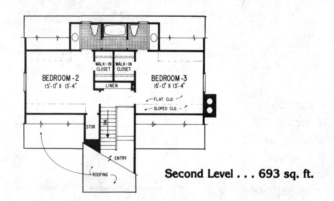

Second Level . . . 693 sq. ft.

First Level . . . 1138 sq. ft.

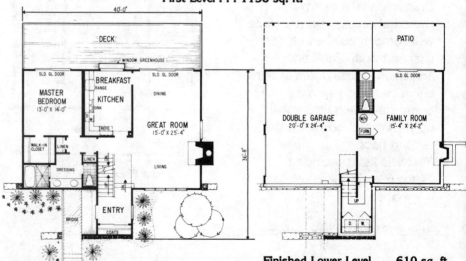

Finished Lower Level . . . 610 sq. ft.

Tri-level home reminiscent of the Colonial era

PLAN 4216

- Strong traditional lines and classic proportions mark this two-story Colonial exterior
- Large family room with laundry facilities, den and powder room are located on entry level
- Living room is five steps up from foyer and features woodburning fireplace
- Three bedrooms and two baths are five more steps up from living room
- L-shaped kitchen with breakfast area has adjacent formal dining room
- Mirror reverse plans available if specified

Designer: Claude Miquelle Associates

Main Levels . . . 1295 sq. ft.

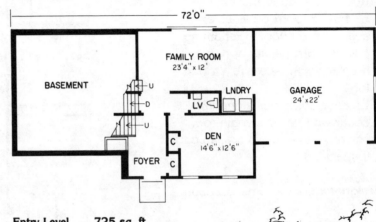

Entry Level . . . 725 sq. ft.

For sites with a fine view

PLAN 3401

- Plan makes the most of a sloping site with a good view
- Entry door opens onto balcony overlooking spectacular two-story living room with rear glass wall
- One whole wing on entry level is devoted to master bedroom suite with private balcony
- Roomy L-shaped balcony off family room provides extra space for outdoor entertaining
- Living room has its own fireplace with recess for storing logs
- Exterior combines stone and cedar with cedar shingle roof
- Mirror reverse plans available if specified

Designer: Elswood-Smith-Carlson

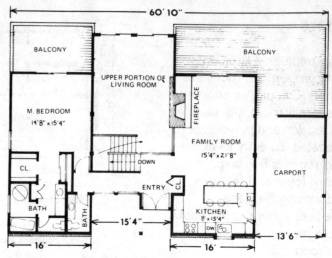

Main Floor . . . 1096 sq. ft.

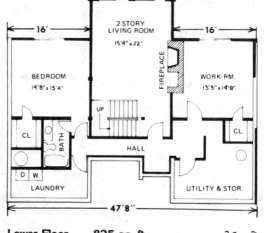

Lower Floor . . . 825 sq. ft.
(finished area)

Well-designed home for the narrow lot

PLAN 3917
PLAN 3917-A (without basement)

- Plenty of deck space and vaulted ceilings over the open living/dining area make the most of limited floor space
- U-shaped kitchen has eating bar that seats three — perfect for the kids
- Master bedroom on upper level has walk-in closet, private deck and bath
- Laundry is strategically placed near kitchen
- Front entry is approached by a protected walkway
- Plan available with or without basement. Please specify
- Materials list costs $20
- Full reverse plans cost an additional $20

Designer: Home Building Plan Service, Inc.

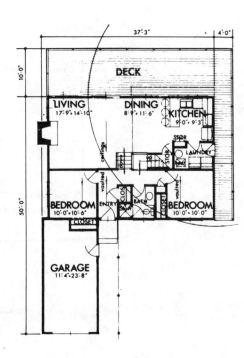

First Floor . . . 936 sq. ft.

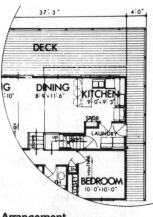

Arrangement
for plan with basement

Second Floor . . . 281 sq. ft.

Architectural detailing in the Colonial tradition

PLAN 6804

- Colonial detailing enhances the exterior of this three-bedroom home
- Living/dining room has excellent view through rear wall of windows and sliding glass door to deck
- Basement level contains a family room with fireplace
- Accessible from the dining room is a large wood deck for easy meals outdoors
- Mirror reverse plans available if specified

Designer: Dave Carmen

Main Level...1,080 sq. ft.

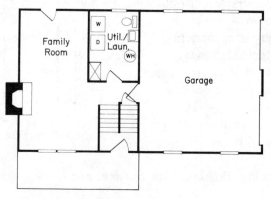

Lower Level...1,008 sq. ft.

Exciting design features cozy conversation pit

PLAN 3224

- Soaring interior ceilings and dramatically angled exterior make this home distinctly contemporary
- Both living room and dining room have vaulted ceilings
- Sunken conversation pit with built-in seating and fireplace is unique feature of main floor
- Luxurious master suite on upper floor has private sun deck, fireplace and large bath with soaking tub, shower and dual vanity with laundry chute
- Also on upper floor is second bedroom and bath
- Materials list costs $10
- Mirror reverse plans available if specified

Designer: L. M. Bruinier

Main Floor . . . 1449 sq. ft.

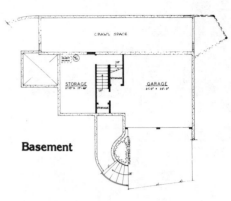

Basement

Upper Level . . . 867 sq. ft.

B. NATHAN.

Family Room Flair

Family room, den, study, library, playroom — however you choose to label it — this room is used for a variety of family activities. How you furnish it depends on the activities which will occur within its walls and who will be using the room — adults, children or both. In many houses the family room is a separate room on the first floor, but it can be located in the basement or in a converted attic, making use of wasted space. You'll have to make sure the area is well heated in the winter and cooled in the summer. Portable heaters and room air conditioners can fulfill these requirements or perhaps you can hook into an existing central system. Because of the hard usage a family room gets, it should be furnished and finished to withstand wear and tear. An easy-to-maintain vinyl flooring may be perfect if eating, drinking and messy craft projects will take place in the room. Or, if television viewing and stereo listening are prime activities, perhaps a sturdy nylon shag rug would provide a more comfortable atmosphere. Paint walls with a heavy-duty enamel and choose durable wallcoverings that are easily cleaned. Furnishing a family room may call for a game table and chairs or perhaps a sofa that converts into a bed, if the room will serve as an auxiliary guest room. The provision of a desk, chair, telephone, adequate lighting and shelving can convert part of the space into a home office. If your family is musical, maybe a piano or organ is in order. The addition of a modular kitchen unit can eliminate trips to the kitchen and provide an excellent place for an informal party. Space allowing, a pool or ping pong table will furnish hours of fun and great exercise on a rainy day. When it comes to lighting, general illumination is desired with task lighting for special functions such as desk work, reading and writing. Task lighting fixtures should be placed so that the light given off is concentrated on the desired spot, and bulbs should be equipped with diffusers or shades to reduce glare and protect eyes. A fireplace in the family room is always a welcome bonus, and helps to set the mood for family togetherness in fun and relaxation.

A family room is just what the name implies — a place where family and friends can gather and enjoy each other's company. In this home the family room is located adjacent to the kitchen and dining area so that the cook can join in on the festivities while preparing meals. Two-story ceiling makes the room appear very large, and a comfortable seating arrangement creates an atmosphere of congeniality.

Photographer: Karl Riek

EXPANSIVE AND DRAMATIC

Left: Here's a large-scale family room ideal for entertaining. A sitting area is located at one end and a game area at the other. The circular stairway leads to a hideaway study/sewing area that overlooks the family room. Sliding glass doors are used to open one area of the room to a roofed and screened outdoor living section. Architect George Van Geldern designed the ceiling with hardwood strip flooring in random widths, and used fixed glass for the clerestory windows.

RETREAT FOR ENTERTAINING

Below: Entertaining guests is an enjoyable task in this festive family room. A complete bar with brass foot rail offers ample storage and refreshment serviceability. Leather-covered bar stools add a look of authenticity. Table in the rear with overhead light provides the perfect spot for your favorite card games or a place to serve snacks to guests or family. A comfortable seating arrangement in the foreground encourages relaxing and friendly conversation.

Photographers: Jim Brett (opposite top); Joshua Freiwald (opposite bottom); Bon Wolter (below)

DESIGNED FOR LEISURE

Right: This family room takes advantage of a horizon-far view with a woodland exposure through fixed windows and sliding glass doors. Even the fireplace is designed to let the outdoors in through a long horizontal window set directly above. Outdoor deck is accessbile through the sliding glass doors, expanding living space. A clean, contemporary look is achieved by using minimum furnishings and ceramic tile for the fireplace surround. Interior design: Helen Marie Logan.

CURL UP WITH A VIEW

Below: Extend your family room to include a conversation pit with built-in seating, fireplace and windows for admiring the view and you've got yourself something special. The one shown here is so inviting that even the family cat would find it hard to turn down as a place for relaxing. Raised, built-in fireplace is framed in diagonal redwood siding for a contemporary look, and the whole area can be illuminated at night by the two overhead spotlights. Designer: Charles Lester, ASID.

FOR THE MUSICALLY INCLINED
Below: Americans love music, and what better place to pursue your favorite pastime than in the family room where friends and relatives can join in listening. This family room overlooks a serene wooded setting and combines piano with fireplace nearby for a relaxed atmosphere. Thick shag carpeting is perfect for flopping on the floor to listen to the magical notes emanating from the piano.

FUSS-FREE INFORMAL LIVING
Opposite: Comfortable seating and a fireplace are almost a must for family rooms. The fabulous room shown here combines these two elements with clean design and natural materials. Beamed dome ceiling soars to a skylight, handsome hearth makes the most of brick, and underfoot there's rugged back-to-nature quarry tile that comes in a wealth of earth hues and decorative shapes. Photo is courtesy of the Tile Council of America.

Photographer: Karl Reik

FAMILY ROOM WITH A SCENIC VIEW
Opposite Top: Love of the outdoors sparked the design for this elegant family room/dining area. The owners have an unobstructed view through the glass of the lovely wooded area surrounding their home. A fireplace, so much a part of every family room, divides the two areas with the added bonus of being open to view on both sides. Contemporary furnishings and hardwood floors provide a luxurious quality to the room.

RUSTIC HIDEAWAY FOR LEISURE ACTIVITIES
Opposite Bottom: There's nothing sterile or antiseptic about this comfortable cove. It's a perfect hideaway spot for playing the grand piano or curling up with a bestseller in front of a crackling fire. The giant fireplace made entirely of stone in random widths and lengths has a cave-like quality and provides plenty of heat to the room. Architectural interest is achieved through the use of wood beams angled toward a central point.

HEART-OF-THE-HOUSE ROOM
Below: Everything you need is right at hand whether you're alone or with family or friends in this intimate family room with adjacent kitchen. One space living makes sense when you have an active, closely-knit family. Handsome wood beams contour to pitched ceiling and are illuminated by recessed lighting for a dramatic effect. Natural flagstone surrounds the fireplace and covers the raised hearth. Glass doors lead outside.

Photographers: Jim Brett (opposite top); Joshua Freiwald (opposite bottom); Ben Wolter (below)

DESIGNED FOR INDIVIDUAL FAMILY ACTIVITIES

Below: Built on a hillside in Sausalito, California, this home's family room interacts with the sunlight and trees. Several different levels segment areas where each family member can pursue his own individual hobby or activity, yet each area is open to the other for a feeling of unity. The lower level where piano is located is topped by a huge 12' by 32' skylight letting in plenty of natural light. Bypassing, sliding doors on this level open to the pool and deck area in the rear. House design: Nantkin & Weber, AIA.

COZY NOOK FOR LEISURE LIVING

Above: There's no rule that says a family room needs to be large. The small room shown above beckons you to curl up with a good book in front of a crackling fire or lounge on the built-in seating to gaze at the beautiful terrain through the many windows. A rustic setting is achieved through the use of wood for ceiling, floor and walls, and stone fireplace appears to have been chipped out of its natural habitat.

WARM AND INVITING ATMOSPHERE

Above: Instead of rigid straight lines and sharp angles, this family room area is a study in gentle curves and circles formed by the custom-designed fireplace hood, the raised hearth, back wall and counter. Easy-care flagstone is used for most of the surface areas. A built-in barbecue to the right of the fireplace lets you enjoy outdoor cooking indoors. Circular cabinet on right provides plenty of space for storage.

Modern home segments bedrooms from active areas

Upper levels... 963 sq. ft.

PLAN 3421

- Elegant half-timbered exterior reflects traditional family living
- Upper level bedrooms assure privacy and quiet
- Formal dining room adds to those special occasions
- Cozy fireplace for intimate family gatherings
- Mirror reverse plans available if specified

Designer: Elswood-Smith-Carlson

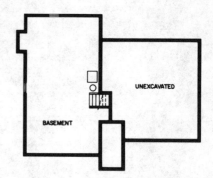

Lower levels... 863 sq. ft.

Split-level design for a rear view

Rear View

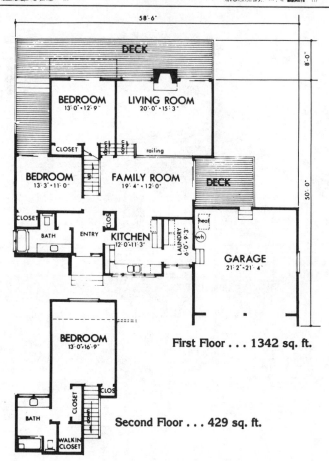

Front View

PLAN 3860

- Perfect for hilltop or waterfront site, this contemporary design features rear glass expanses and plenty of deck space
- Overhanging second floor bedroom has full bath plus three closets
- Roomy kitchen opens into family room with adjoining dining deck, and is accessible from garage through laundry room
- Open railing at the front end of the living room permits fireplace and rear view to be seen from the family room
- Materials list costs $20
- Full reverse plans cost an additional $20

Designer: Home Building Plan Service, Inc.

DECK

BEDROOM
13'·0"·12'·9"

LIVING ROOM
20'·0"·15'·3"

CLOSET

railing

BEDROOM
13'·3"·11'·0"

FAMILY ROOM
19'·4"·12'·0"

DECK

CLOSET

BATH

ENTRY

KITCHEN
12'·0"·11'·3"

LAUNDRY
6'·0"·9'·3"

heat

GARAGE
21'·2"·21'·4"

58'·6"

8'·0"

50'·0"

First Floor . . . 1342 sq. ft.

BEDROOM
13'·0"·16'·9"

CLOSET

CLOS

BATH

WALK IN CLOSET

Second Floor . . . 429 sq. ft.

For leisure living at its best

PLAN 7505

- Distinctive variation of the popular A-frame
- Entire front facade is glass permitting excellent view potential
- Living/dining room has vaulted ceiling and fireplace
- L-shaped deck is perfect for sun worshippers
- Master bedroom is located on first level in rear for added privacy
- Circular stairway leads to two second floor bedrooms and bath
- Materials list is included
- Mirror reverse plans available if specified

Designer: National Home Planning Service

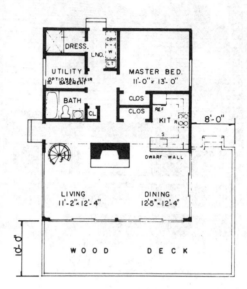

First Level . . . 962 sq. ft.

Second Level . . . 578 sq. ft.

English Tudor exudes charm

PLAN 3632

- Charming English Tudor adaptation with contemporary floor plan
- Living room features wood-burning fireplace, square bay window and ornamental iron railing running along stairway and entry
- Formal dining room opens onto elevated wood deck through sliding glass doors
- Huge family room on lower level also has fireplace
- Plan has three bedrooms and two-and-a-half baths
- Materials list is included
- Full reverse plans available if specified

Designer: Garlinghouse

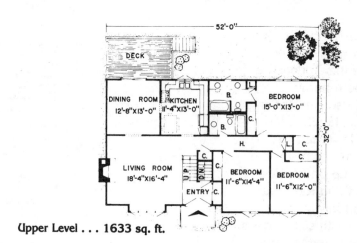

Upper Level . . . 1633 sq. ft.

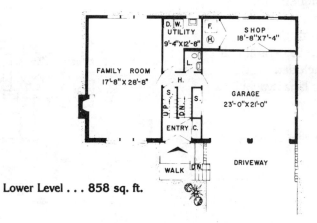

Lower Level . . . 858 sq. ft.

Distinguished styling with split-level convenience

PLAN 2064

- Stucco, adzed timber, brick and slate are primary exterior elements of this Tudor-style, three-bedroom home
- Lower level also contains small den or office, family room opening to lower terrace, laundry room and bathroom
- Three steps up on left side of house is living room with fireplace and bay window, dining room with sliding glass doors to upper terrace and well-planned kitchen with breakfast area
- Upper level has three bedrooms open to central hall
- Materials list included
- Mirror reverse plans available if specified

Designer: Master Plan Service

Lower Level . . . 466 sq. ft.

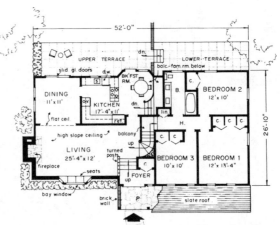

Upper Level . . . 1336 sq. ft.

Excitingly modern plan has delightful "penthouse" master bedroom

PLAN 2648

- Dramatic open interior spaces and clean lines highlight this contemporary plan
- Upper floor is devoted to delightful "penthouse" master bedroom suite with private deck
- Main floor features two decks accessible from breakfast room and living room
- Dining room is open to living room with fireplace and has exciting greenhouse window
- Materials list is included
- Mirror reverse plans available if specified

Designer: John D. Bloodgood, AIA

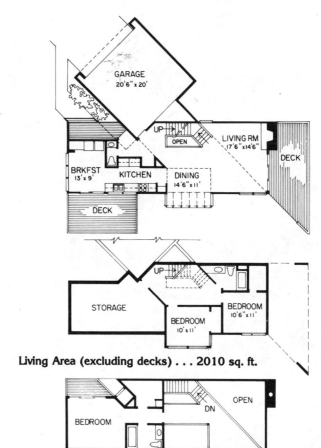

Living Area (excluding decks) . . . 2010 sq. ft.

Exciting contemporary with an emphasis on family living

Plan 6803

- Large wrap-around deck has access from living and dining areas
- Family kitchen makes use of space by adding counter seating and spacious dining area
- Sunken living area is set off with wood railing and attractive circular steps
- Mirror reverse plans available if specified

Designer: Dave Carmen

Living Area...1,180 sq. ft.

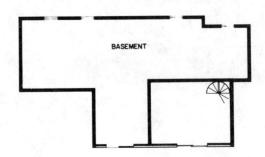

Beautifully modern plan for side-sloping lot

PLAN 3949

- Aesthetically pleasing exterior design features cathedral windows and angled entry porch
- Three bedrooms and two baths on one side of entry hall, away from active living areas
- Spacious kitchen has extra counterspace and a storage closet
- Living/dining room with vaulted ceiling features clerestory windows for natural toplighting
- Angled fireplace is visible from the entry, and an adjacent side deck adds living space
- Materials list costs $20
- Full reverse plans cost an additional $20

Designer: Home Building Plan Service, Inc.

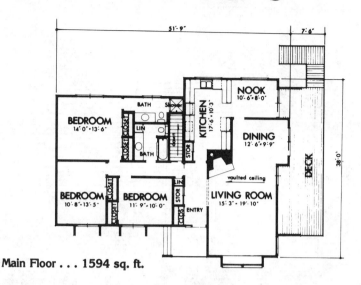

Main Floor . . . 1594 sq. ft.

Basement

Excellent design for the smaller family

PLAN 3337

- Vertical wood siding, stone and extra high windows accent the exterior of this classic design
- Well-designed floor plan is compact and convenient
- Lower level has extra-large bedroom with full bath and utility room in rear
- Gigantic family room on main floor enjoys access to rear patio and boasts corner fireplace
- Specify foundation option: full basement, crawlspace or slab
- Materials list costs $10
- Mirror reverse plans available if specified

Designer: W. L. Corley

Main Floor . . . 1173 sq. ft.

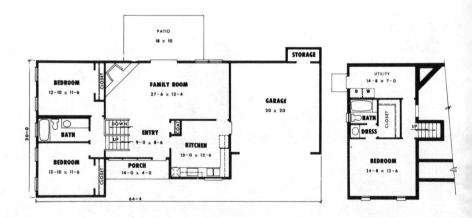

Lower Floor . . . 480 sq. ft

Maximum livability in modest, compact home

PLAN 4214

- Diamond-pane windows add a touch of warmth and comfort to this plan's exterior
- All three bedrooms are located over the garage in one side of house for maximum privacy
- Main level contains huge living room with fireplace, U-shaped kitchen with access to porch, and formal dining room
- Mirror reverse plans available if specified

Designer: Claude Miquelle Associates

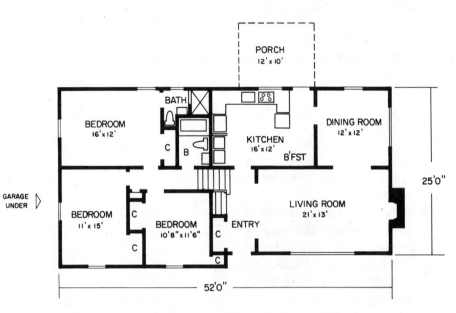

Main Floor . . . 1353 sq. ft.

Basement

Variations on a contemporary theme

PLAN 3858 (with standard basement)
PLAN 3858-A (without basement)
PLAN 3858-B (with daylight basement)

- Low, contemporary lines of exterior ideal for sloping lot, especially with rear view
- Living room with fireplace opens out onto wood deck
- Master bedroom on upper level has private deck, bath, walk-in wardrobe, and receives natural lighting from clerestory windows
- Plan 3858-B with daylight basement includes extra bedroom with walk-in closet and bath, plus recreation room and large general use room
- Specify with or without basement, standard or daylight
- Materials list costs $20
- Full reverse plans cost an additional $20

Designer: Home Building Plan Service, Inc.

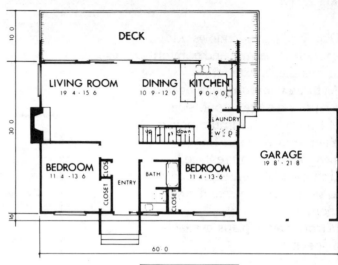

Living Area (without basement) . . . 1535 sq. ft.

Basement

Front View

Optimum living on two levels

PLAN 2254

- Spacious sunken living room with extended window section for panoramic view
- Walk-in pantry and utility area off kitchen and breakfast areas
- Three bedrooms and two baths on main level; bedroom, bath, family room and storage area on lower level
- Dramatic sloped ceilings in kitchen/breakfast area, dining and living rooms
- Materials list included; full reverse plans available for an additional $30

Designer: National Plan Service

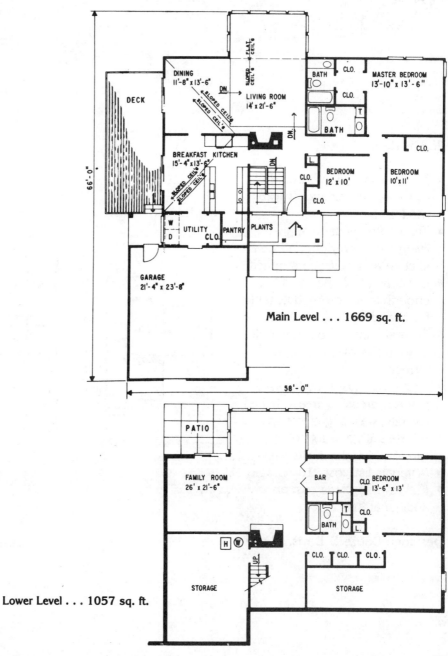

Main Level . . . 1669 sq. ft.

Lower Level . . . 1057 sq. ft.

Elegant home with lots of street appeal

PLAN 4048

- Multi-levels and interesting rooflines add exterior flair to modern plan
- Tiled entry leads to sunken living room on right and den, kitchen and bedrooms on left
- Kitchen is L-shaped and big enough to accommodate table for breakfast
- Formal dining room has wall of windows overlooking rear terrace
- Secluded master bedroom features dressing area with dual lavanity, wall-long closet space, private bath and lots of windows to take in the view
- Materials list cost $10
- Full reverse plans cost an additional $10

Designer: Danze & Davis, AIA

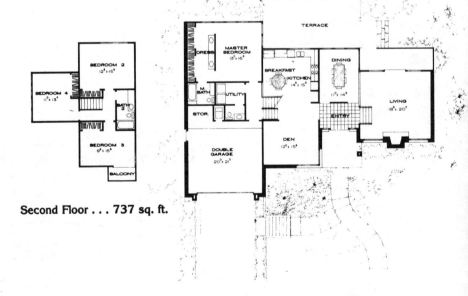

Second Floor . . . 737 sq. ft.

First Floor . . . 1583 sq. ft.

Home for a tight-knit family

PLAN 2749

- Clean, modern styling with excellent interior floor plan
- Three bedrooms and two baths are isolated in right wing of home
- Master bedroom enjoys sloped ceiling and private deck accessible through sliding glass doors
- Sunken great room is divided from dining room by railings
- U-shaped kitchen has built-in booth for informal meals
- Large rear deck can be reached from dining room or kitchen for outdoor entertaining
- Laundry and storage is behind two-car garage
- Materials list included
- Mirror reverse plans available if specified

Designer: Henry D. Norris, AIA

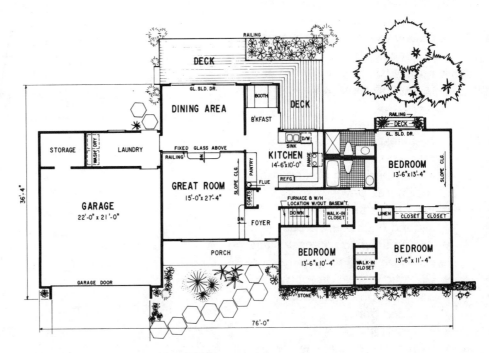

Living Area . . . 1502 sq. ft.

Luxury with a French accent

PLAN 6407

- Stately exterior is reminiscent of French chateau style
- Family room, living room and recreation room all have fireplaces
- Charming bay window in breakfast area overlooks large rear wood deck
- Master bedroom on first floor maximizes privacy
- Four large bedrooms on second floor share a bath
- Two unfinished rooms upstairs could be used for storage
- Gigantic recreation room and bath on lower floor is added bonus
- Materials list costs $5
- Mirror reverse plans available if specified

Designer: Homes by Helm

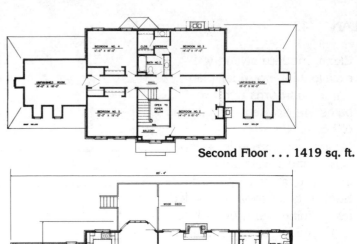

Second Floor . . . 1419 sq. ft.

First Floor . . . 2013 sq. ft.

Basement . . . 815 sq. ft.

Rustic home ideal for wooded site

Rear view

PLAN 3813
PLAN 3813-A (without basement)

- Rustic exterior has roof of handsplit and resawn cedar shakes, built for heavy snow loads
- Living/dining area with vaulted ceiling juts out onto spacious rear deck and brings the outdoors in through windows and sliding glass doors
- Both plans have three main floor bedrooms; the basement (plan 3813) has an additional bedroom and bath, plus a divided recreation room with masonry fireplace
- Plan is available with or without basement. Please specify
- Materials list costs $20
- Full reverse plans cost an additional $20

Designer: Home Building Plan Service, Inc.

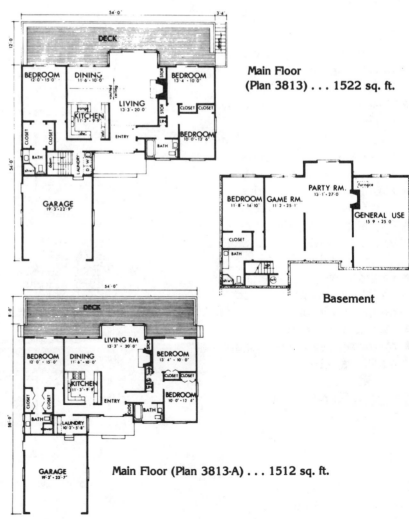

Main Floor
(Plan 3813) . . . 1522 sq. ft.

Basement

Main Floor (Plan 3813-A) . . . 1512 sq. ft.

A plan to reflect your personality and interests

PLAN 2347

- Exterior of contemporary split-level is brick veneer and wood siding covered by three hip roofs
- Spacious foyer leads directly to all major zones of house
- Open stair with planter on one side leads to three bedrooms and a spacious main bath
- Master bedroom includes private bath with shower
- Family room with wall of windows overlooks rear patio on ground floor level
- Laundry, two additional rooms and third full bath are also on ground level
- Materials list is included
- Mirror reverse plans cost an additional $10

Designer: Samuel Paul, AIA

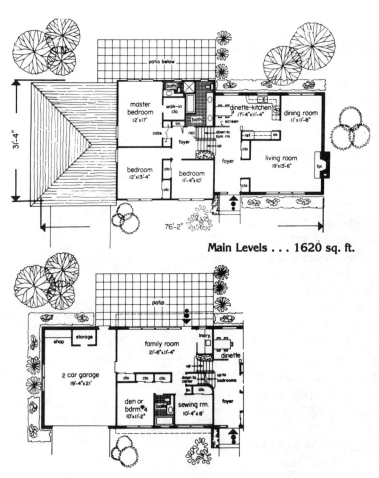

Main Levels . . . 1620 sq. ft.

Lower Level . . . 702 sq. ft.

Specially designed to tame a sloping lot

PLAN 2649

- Split-entry plan utilizes land to best advantage
- Long, low rooflines visually tie the house to its site and provide lots of upper level living space
- Entry level living room has vaulted ceiling up to dining-kitchen balcony
- Three bedrooms and two baths on upper level
- Lower level provides garage, family room with fireplace, storage area, and bonus room for guests or hobby use
- Materials list is included
- Mirror reverse plans available if specified

Designer: John D. Bloodgood, AIA

Patio 24×8
Br 1 15×12
Dining 11×14-6
K/Brkfst 11×14-6
Br 2 11-6×11-6
Br 3 9×11-6
Lr 15-6×14-6
dn up
50'
37-6'

Living Area . . . 2157 sq. ft.

Bonus 11-6×14-6
Family 22×14-6
W D
up dn
Mechanical
Storage 15×14-6
Gar 23×21
Unexcav.

Bathroom Beauties

Today's bath is more stylish, dramatic and colorful than ever before. It is no longer a utility room. The fact is, the bathroom is now establishing its identity as more than a place where all the plumbing pipes come together. As the kitchen has evolved from a place of drudgery to an actual retreat, so today's bath may be not only a place to brush one's teeth, but also one in which to relax, even to revel. The little, cramped room, hidden away and preferably not even mentioned, has become the most individualistic, most displayed room of all. More than anything else, the ordinary bath suffers from a lack of planning, resulting in a generally unharmonious look. The glaring problems this produces include lack of simple comforts — a place to sit down, a place to put things, fixtures and fittings at awkward heights, inadequate lighting for grooming, poor ventilation, insufficient electrical outlets, lack of storage for towels, and medicine cabinets without locks and too small for many cosmetics. The rule of thumb today is better one adequate, even luxurious bath in a house, with a half-bath somewhere for convenience, than two or three cramped, purely utilitarian standard baths. The result is glamour galore, a room that bespeaks your personality and exudes creature comforts. And thanks to today's incredible variety of fixtures, linens and accessories you can create a bathroom beauty that is unique and multi-functional. Lots of natural light, space for extra shelves, attention to the needs of both sexes, a second washbasin, good artificial lighting, more and larger mirrors, provision for storage and use of hair dryers, etc., are all amenities that you should strive for in your new bath. After all, the average cost of a bathroom per square foot is higher than any other room in the house, so this rates some careful planning and attention to detail.

This beautiful room incorporates many exciting, contemporary design features typical of today's modern bath. A feeling of warmth is achieved by the use of wall-to-wall carpeting, diagonal redwood siding as a wall treatment and overhead skylights that let in natural light. Large tub is surrounded by wood with a built-in planter on one side making it an inviting place to soak away your troubles. Molded fiberglass shower is attractive and easy to care for.

TOTAL LINGERING BATH ENJOYMENT

Right: A striking combination of mirrors, tile and ultra-modern fixtures along with lots of plants and well-appointed accessories make this a classic for those who prefer a contemporary look. Recessed soffit lighting illuminates the room at night, while overhead skylight provides natural light during the day. Oversized oval soaking tub has built-in seat. Fixtures are by American Standard and come in a variety of colors.

SHOWERING IN THE SUNLIGHT

Below Left: Today's technology has provided us with an easy-care material called fiberglass that can be used in a variety of ways. Here, we see it in a moulded, one-piece shower with corner seat and gold-trimmed door. If you've always wondered what it would be like to shower outside, this bath design can give you a fairly close idea. Skylight directly over the shower practically brings the outdoors inside. Shower is by American Standard.

A TASTE OF THE ORIENT

Below Right: This bath, with an oriental flavor, is compartmented with sliding doors for complete privacy. The soaking tub is available for a luxurious bath or shower. There is also a shower between the tub area and vanity area. Stepping stones of flagstone are set into a bed of rounded stones for contrasting texture. Access to this area may be gained from a door to the right leading to the swimming pool. Ceramic tile is from American Olean.

Photographers: Jim Brett (lower left), John Hartley (lower right)

A TOUCH OF CHARM

Left: New home baths need not have plain, dull white walls. Brick panels were used along with a variety of space-saving fixtures to create an illusion of space and charm in this 6 x 8-foot bathroom. The brick-like fiberglass reinforced panels add a durable and imaginative note to the bath. The non-porous surface can be easily cleaned with a damp cloth and never needs painting. Brick panels are made by Marlite.

VAULTED CEILING GIVES SENSE OF SPACE

Below Left: A smaller bath achieves the feeling of a larger one with vaulted ceilings that soar upward. Large windows let in natural light and take advantage of the view. Horizontal wood siding applied to the walls gives a rustic appearance and blends well with the tile floor. Creative use of mirrors and bulb lights makes an attractive wall behind the dual lavanity.

ENJOY RELAXING IN A GREENHOUSE BATH

Below Right: Limited space is no deterent to creating a garden bath as this room so well indicates. The tub is enclosed on one side with a sliding glass door which opens to a wood-decked patio-greenhouse built of redwood, complete with lattice roof. Redwood slats frame the mirror and are used for the wall surfacing above the vanity, adding to the indoor/outdoor character of this small, attractive bath. Designer: Rod Tucker

ADD A DASH OF THEATRICS

Below Left: Innovative use of ceramic tile can add a different dimension to a modern bath design. A ribbon of crimson tile bordered by tiny lights sweeps down the wall, over the tub and up the other side. Beautiful ebony tub provides lots of space to soak and relax. Wall-to-wall carpeting covers the floor and steps to the right for warmth underfoot, while plants and elegant accessories give a luxurious look to the room. Bath design: Interpace.

CREATING A FOCAL POINT

Below Right: A bath nook for the lady of the house is built around a sunken tub of oval design for luxurious bathing. The step-up tile design is extended to convenient ledges at each end of the tub and to the recessed storage area which features a trio of glass shelves and recessed lighting niche. Paneling is used for other walls of this room as well as for the archway which frames the setting. Bath design: American Olean Tile Co.

THE ULTIMATE IN LUXURY

Opposite Top: What could be more intimate than your very own whirlpool in the bathroom. Feeling the thousands of tiny air bubbles bursting against your skin, creating a warm tingling massasge, induces the deep relaxation your body needs. The bath shown here comes in nine different sizes from a standard single to a spacious family size model. And they can be color coordinated to match your bath's decor. This whirlpool is from Viking Sauna Co.

WARM THE BATHROOM WITH WOOD

Opposite Bottom: This unusual masculine bath retreat showcases a line of fiberglass bath fixtures and decorative hardware available from LeTrone International of Los Angeles. Horizontal knotty pine siding treated with a wood sealant is used for a rustic looking wallcovering. Spotlights illuminate the bath area and mirror. Hardware is made of pewter, and the mirror over the sink is polished brass.

Photographer: Harold Davis

Hillside charmer is great for entertaining or casual living

PLAN 3923

- Perfect for a growing family, this modest-sized home has three bedrooms in upstairs wing, plus an extra bedroom and bath below
- Both living room and the recreation room in the daylight basement have fireplaces
- Serving bar between roomy kitchen and nook makes family meals convenient, while deck off the dining room allows outdoor meals
- Living room opens onto another deck in front via sliding glass doors, adding outdoor living space
- Plenty of built-in storage
- Materials list costs $20
- Full reverse plans cost an additional $20

Designer: Home Building Plan Service, Inc.

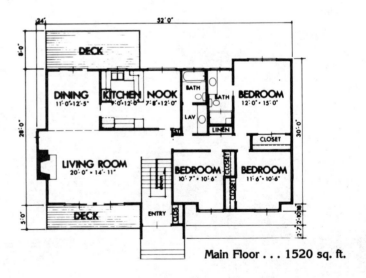

Main Floor . . . 1520 sq. ft.

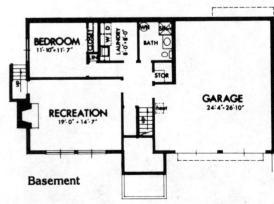

Basement

Small and simple plan with a view

PLAN 3948

- Simple exterior design and a practical interior make this small plan a good choice for either a second or year-round home
- Three decks provide easy access to the fresh outdoor air
- One of the three bedrooms may be used as a den, depending on your needs
- Kitchen has convenient eating counter, and laundry space is close at hand
- Garage spans full width of house for storage of both car and boat if required
- Materials list costs $20
- Full reverse plans cost an additional $20

Designer: Home Building Plan Service, Inc.

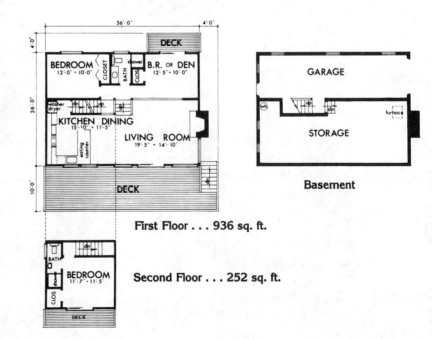

First Floor ... 936 sq. ft.

Second Floor ... 252 sq. ft.

Basement

PLAN 3909
PLAN 3909-A (without basement)

- Clerestory windows, vaulted ceilings and a second floor balcony create bold interior spaces
- Side deck adjoins living room via sliding glass doors
- Fireplace in living room with sleekly styled chimney exterior
- Long window at stairway landing has striking visual impact
- One bedroom and full bath on first floor; two more bedrooms and a bath upstairs
- U-shaped kitchen opens into two-story-high living room area
- Plan available with or without basement. Please specify
- Materials list costs $20
- Full reverse plans cost an additional $20

Designer: Home Building Plan Service, Inc.

Second Floor . . . 517 sq. ft.

First Floor . . . 946 sq. ft.

Holiday look with year-round spaciousness

Luxury living on multi-levels

PLAN 3908 (with family room)
PLAN 3908-A (with dining room)

- Both plans feature three bedrooms, living room with fireplace, daylight basement with recreation and utility rooms, and wood deck
- U-shaped kitchen in Plan 3908 opens into a family room
- Plan 3908-A has kitchen adjoining dining room for more formal eating
- Six stairs lead from double-door entry to first floor level
- Laundry room conveniently located near kitchen
- Picture windows and deck are designed for a sloping lot with front orientation
- Specify desired plan precisely
- Materials list costs $20
- Full reverse plans cost an additional $20

Designer: Home Building Plan Service, Inc.

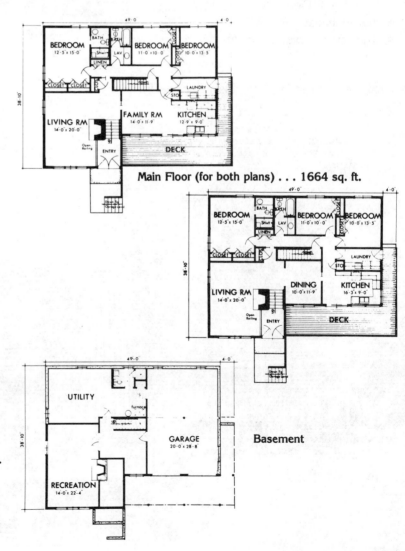

Main Floor (for both plans) . . . 1664 sq. ft.

Basement

Vacation plan offers four decks, optional basement

PLAN 3816
PLAN 3816-A (without basement)

- A spacious 1640 square feet of living area, plus four large decks for outdoor living space
- Of three bedrooms, two measure a full 15'9"x13'
- One full bath on main level plus a bath and dressing room off the master suite
- U-shaped kitchen includes eating counter between kitchen and dining areas
- High-ceilinged living room has masonry fireplace constructed with 6" concrete blocks and 4" stone facing
- Plan available with or without basement. Please specify
- Materials list costs $20
- Full reverse plans cost an additional $20

Designer: Home Building Plan Service, Inc.

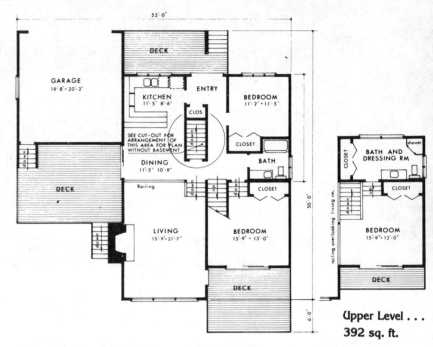

Main Floor . . . 1248 sq. ft.

Upper Level . . . 392 sq. ft.

Arrangement of laundry for plan without basement

Tailor made for today's family

PLAN 3631

- Contemporary home blends well with natural surroundings
- Natural battened plywood siding is complemented by light red brick trim and stained exposed beams
- Main level has three bedrooms and two baths
- Compact kitchen is open to family room and sliding glass doors provide access to elevated wood deck
- Recreation room, another bedroom and bath, two patios and shop/storage space are on lower level
- Materials list is included
- Full reverse plans available if specified

Designer: Garlinghouse

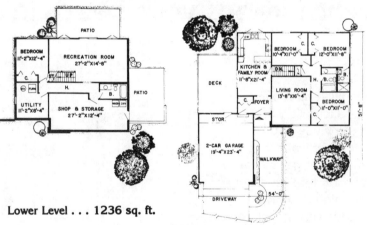

Lower Level . . . 1236 sq. ft.

First Floor . . . 1236 sq. ft.

Plan that keeps your needs in mind

PLAN 2348

- Soaring split-level roofline and dramatic gallery are enhanced by use of brick veneer and vertical siding
- 285 square foot gallery can be used for future expansion
- Two-story-high entrance portico adds sense of glamour
- Gracious reception foyer is highlighted by brick walls, one a full two stories, one formed by back of fireplace in living room
- Efficient kitchen and dinette overlook rear garden
- Lower level has family room and wrap-around deck
- Materials list is included
- Mirror reverse plans cost an additional $10

Designer: Samuel Paul, AIA

Main Level . . . 1527 sq. ft.

Upper Level . . . 285 sq. ft.

Lower Level . . . 488 sq. ft.

Ultra-contemporary with design integrity

PLAN 2748

- Designed for a view lot, contemporary home combines shingles, stone and wood
- Luxurious master bedroom on main floor has its own fireplace, access to rear deck, private bath and dressing area
- Clerestory windows add natural light to the two-story living room and open hallway
- Kitchen is conveniently located between breakfast room and formal dining room
- Second floor has three additional bedrooms and two baths; two of the bedrooms have private decks
- Materials list is included
- Mirror reverse plans available if specified

Designer: Henry D. Norris, AIA

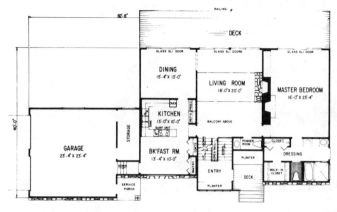

First Floor . . . 1809 sq. ft.

Second Floor . . . 1293 sq. ft.

Country charmer appeals to sense of tradition

PLAN 2425

- Charming Colonial has well-designed interior plan
- Spacious first floor living room features traditional bay window, fireplace and access to rear covered porch
- Informal living room has unusual corner fireplace and is open to U-shaped kitchen
- Additional room adjacent to kitchen can be used as fourth bedroom or den
- Covered porch connects garage with utility room and workshop
- Second floor has three bedrooms, two of which open onto rear balcony/deck
- Mirror reverse plans available if specified

Designer: William M. Thompson, AIA

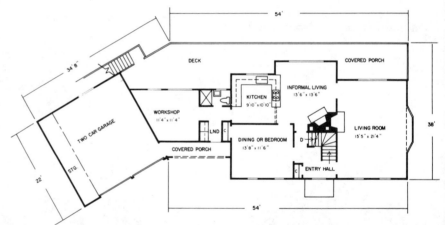

First Floor . . . 1140 sq. ft.

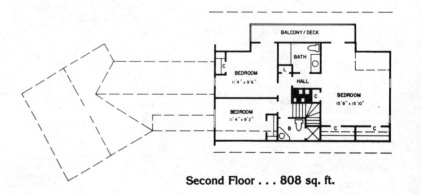

Second Floor . . . 808 sq. ft.

Hillside split-level features wide rear deck

PLAN 3941

- Rear orientation of this design is underlined by full-length, 12-foot-wide rear deck
- Kitchen/dining/living area is on sunken level; bedroom with bath and den are on entry level
- Between living room and den are built-in bookcases, and both ceilings are vaulted
- Den opens out onto side deck via sliding glass doors
- Second floor bedroom features walk-in closet and private deck, plus bath
- A third bedroom and bath, plus recreation room are located in basement
- Materials list costs $20
- Full reverse plans cost an additional $20

Designer: Home Building Plan Service, Inc.

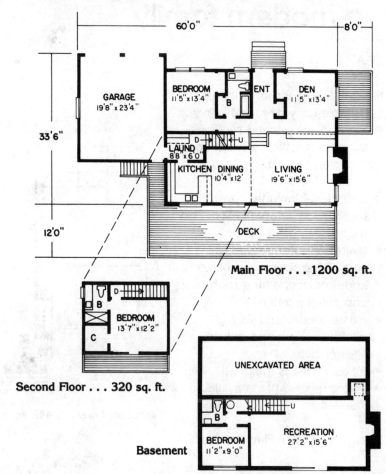

Main Floor . . . 1200 sq. ft.

Second Floor . . . 320 sq. ft.

Basement

B·NATHAN

Interior room arrangement geared for a modern family

PLAN 2061

- This three-bedroom home is suitable for year-round living
- Plan boasts pitched rooflines, tall windows, two-story entrance tower and elevated decks for a soaring look
- Entry level includes foyer, family room, laundry room and mud room
- Main living consists of two-story living room with balcony and fireplace, dining room and eat-in kitchen
- Master bedroom has high pitched ceiling and private shower bath
- Materials list is included
- Mirror reverse plans available if specified

Designer: Master Plan Service

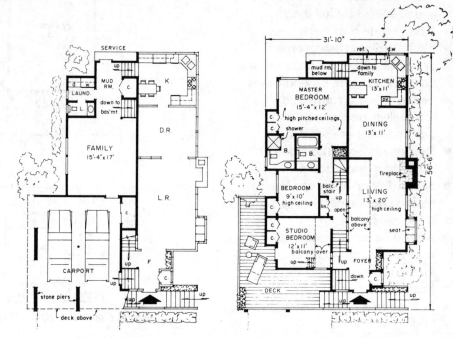

Lower Level . . . 442 sq. ft.

Main Levels . . . 1412 sq. ft.

A home to suit any neighborhood

PLAN 4049

- This plan offers plenty of space for a growing family
- Tiled entry leads up to spacious living/dining room which is separated by a fireplace
- Efficient kitchen has eat-in space for informal meals
- Two bedrooms and bath complete this level
- Upper floor is devoted to the master bedroom suite with raised area for bed, sitting area and plenty of closet space
- Lower floor includes fourth bedroom with bath, large play room and hobby room
- Rear deck spans living/dining room and lets outdoors in through lots of windows
- Materials list costs $10
- Full reverse plans cost an additional $10

Designer: Danze & Davis

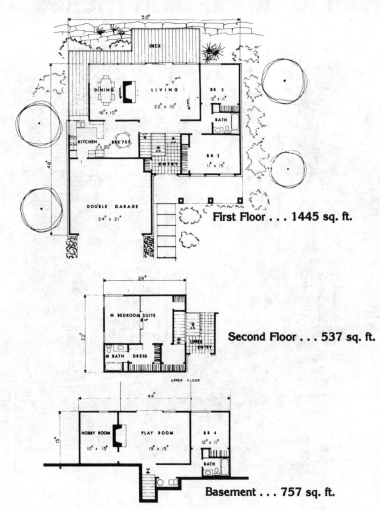

First Floor . . . 1445 sq. ft.

Second Floor . . . 537 sq. ft.

Basement . . . 757 sq. ft.

PLAN 3869
PLAN 3869-A (without basement)

- Unusual ship's bow wood deck in rear is perfect for scenic outdoor living
- Sliding glass doors adjoin living room, dining room and master bedroom to deck
- Extended two-story living room with fireplace is overlooked by recreation room on upper level
- Clerestory windows insure plenty of natural light
- Private decks are accessible to two upper level bedrooms
- Plenty of storage space, including two walk-in closets
- Materials list costs $20
- Full reverse plans cost an additional $20

Designer: Home Building Plan Service, Inc.

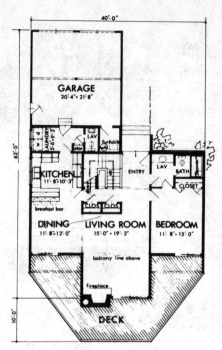

First Floor ... 1216 sq. ft.

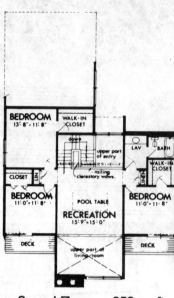

Second Floor ... 958 sq. ft.

Basement ... 810 sq. ft.

Note: Illustration shows rear view of plan with basement.

Hillside home plan makes the most of view

Bi-level living for a view lot

PLAN 2130

- Two-level design makes optimum use of glass across rear and side of three-bedroom home
- Sunken master bedroom, family room and living room have sliding glass doors opening to rear deck
- Fireplaces enhance both master bedroom and living room with elegant conversation pit
- Family room features refreshment bar with sink
- Entry-level dining room is raised above living room, creating a balcony effect
- Materials list costs $15
- Mirror reverse plans available if specified

Designer: Ron Dick

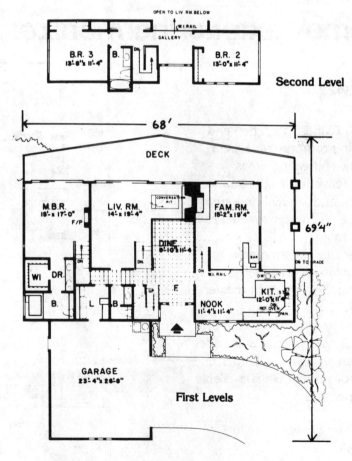

Living Area . . . 2474 sq. ft.

Home's exterior harmonizes with inclined site

Plan 3422

- Two islands in kitchen and dining room provide extra work and eating areas
- Attractive foyer opens onto deck and family living areas
- Deck off master suite takes advantage of hillside view
- Spacious dressing area, double sinks, and large wardrobes highlight master bath
- Third level provides room for family growth and a large rec room with built-in fireplace
- Mirror reverse plans available if specified

Designer: Elswood-Smith-Carlson

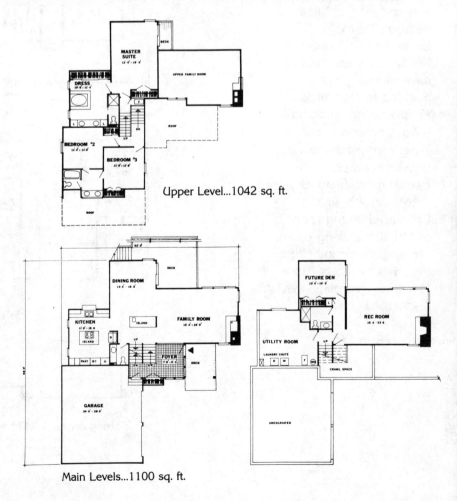

Upper Level...1042 sq. ft.

Main Levels...1100 sq. ft.

Visual sharing of interior spaces

PLAN 4050

- Modern home fits snugly into sloping lot
- A sense of openness is achieved by combining the living room with dining room and the kitchen with family room
- Living/dining room has excellent view through rear wall of windows and sliding glass door to deck
- Family room and two-story living room have fireplaces
- Upper floor has four bedrooms and two baths including extra-large master bedroom suite with lots of closet space
- Materials list costs $10
- Full reverse plans cost an additional $10

Designer: Danze & Davis

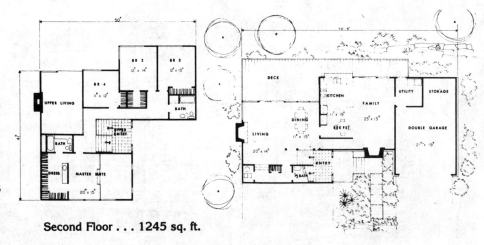

Second Floor . . . 1245 sq. ft.

First Floor . . . 1345 sq. ft.

Modern home lets your personality show

PLAN 5205

- Striking lines and unusual-shaped windows provide unique look to three-bedroom plan
- Over-sized living room with fireplace has interesting spiral staircase leading to two bedrooms on upper level
- Bay window adds charm to dining room
- Master bedroom is isolated in rear of home on main level
- Lower level includes game room and storage/workshop
- L-shaped deck surrounds living room
- Mirror reverse plans cost an additional $3

Designer: Worthman Homes, Inc.

Basement . . . 856 sq. ft.

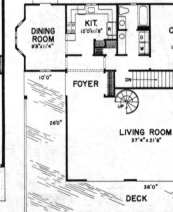

Living Area . . . 2314 sq. ft.

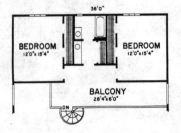

Vacation home with options

PLAN 3844
Alternates available
Specify precisely

- Your choice of standard basement, no basement, or a daylight basement with car and boat garage plus two extra rooms
- A second floor balcony overlooks the extended two-story living room with fireplace
- Alternate plans offer options of large dormitory on upper level, or third bedroom with bath
- Wrap-around deck assures optimum sun and view potential
- Plenty of closets and storage space for vacation gear
- Materials list costs $20
- Full reverse plans cost an additional $20

Designer: Home Building
Plan Service, Inc.

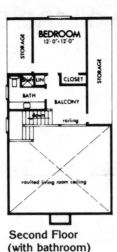

Second Floor
(with bathroom)
. . . 336 sq. ft.

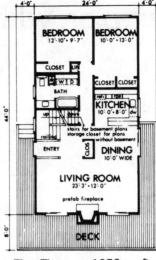

First Floor . . . 1056 sq. ft.

Second Floor
(without bathroom)
. . . 336 sq. ft.

FOR PLAN WITH NO BASEMENT
AND BEDROOM/BATH ON SECOND FLOOR
PLAN 3844-1A
FOR PLAN WITH NO BASEMENT
AND DORMITORY ON SECOND FLOOR
PLAN 3844-2A
FOR PLAN WITH STANDARD BASEMENT
AND BEDROOM/BATH ON SECOND FLOOR
PLAN 3844-1B
FOR PLAN WITH STANDARD BASEMENT
AND DORMITORY ON SECOND FLOOR
PLAN 3844-2B
FOR PLAN WITH DAYLIGHT BASEMENT
AND BEDROOM/BATH ON SECOND FLOOR
PLAN 3844-1C
FOR PLAN WITH DAYLIGHT BASEMENT
AND DORMITORY ON SECOND FLOOR
PLAN 3844-2C

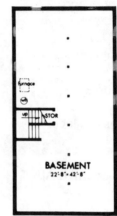

Standard Basement

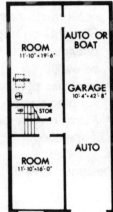

Daylight Basement

Spectacular plan with all the extras

PLAN 6703

- Deck space abounds in modern home for outdoor living enjoyment
- L-shaped kitchen is high-lighted by butcher block island, greenhouse, built-in grill and breakfast deck outside
- Entertainment space abounds in living room and recreation room with complete bar facilities, dancing area and see-through fireplace
- Skylights on upper level provide natural light to entry below
- Roof has observation and sunning deck
- Mirror reverse plans available if specified

Designer: Edward A. Schmitt, AIA

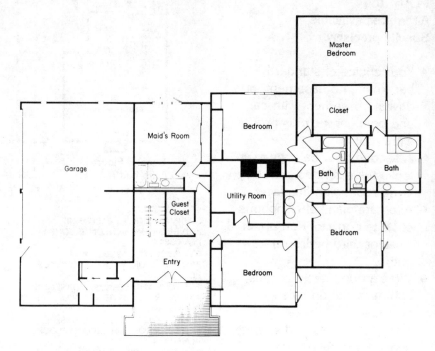

Upper Level . . . 2254 sq. ft.
First Level . . . 2552 sq. ft.

Spacious living area ideal for entertaining

PLAN 4110

- Excellent plan for a vacation or year-round home on a view site
- Three wood decks provide lots of outdoor living space
- Exposed beams run through family room, kitchen, living room and dining room
- Sunken family room has built-in fireplace with extended hearth
- Lower level offers extra-large recreation room with fireplace and refreshment center
- Fourth bedroom and shop are also on lower level
- Materials list costs $5
- Mirror reverse plans available if specified

Designer: Sam Benedict

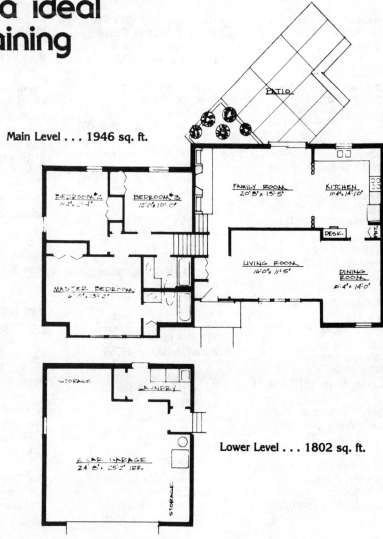

Main Level . . . 1946 sq. ft.

Lower Level . . . 1802 sq. ft.

Manufacturers' Index

Appliances

Amana Refrigeration, Inc.
Amana, IA 52204

Caloric Corp.
18444 West 10 Mile Rd.
Topton, PA 19562

Distinctive Appliances, Inc.
8820 Lankershim Blvd.
Sun Valley, CA 91352

Frigidaire Div.,
General Motors Corp.
300 Taylor St.
Dayton, OH 45442

General Electric
2100 Gardiner Ln.
Louisville, KY 40205

Hardwick Stove Co.
240 Edward St.
Cleveland, TN 37311

Hotpoint Div., GE Co.
2100 Gardiner Ln.
Louisville, KY 40205

In-Sink-Erator Div.,
Emerson Electric Co.
4700 21st St.
Racine, WI 53406

Jenn-Air Corp.
3035 N. Shadeland Ave.
Indianapolis, IN 46226

Magic Chef, Inc.
Box 717
Cleveland, TN 37311

Maytag Company
Newton, IA 50208

Modern Maid, Div.
McGraw-Edison Co.
Box 1111
Chattanooga, TN 37401

Monarch Range Co.
715 N. Spring St.
Beaver Dam, WI 53916

Norris Industries, Thermador/Waste King Div.
5119 District Blvd.
Los Angeles, CA 90022

Ronson Corp.
One Ronson Rd.
Woodbridge, NJ 07095

Tappan Appliance Corp.
Tappan Park
Mansfield, OH 44901

Whirlpool Corp.
Benton Harbor, MI 49022

Bath Fixtures & Fittings

American Standard, Inc.
P. O. Box 2003
New Brunswick, NJ 08903

Belwood Div.
U. S. Industries, Inc.
Ackerman, MS 39735

Bradley Corp.
Box 348
Menomonee Falls, WI 53051

Delta Faucet Co.
Box 31
Greensburg, IN 47240

Eljer Plumbingware Div.
Wallace-Murray Corp.
3 Gateway Center
Pittsburg, PA 15222

General Bathroom
Products Corp.
2201 Touhy Ave.
Elk Grove Village, IL 60007

Hallmack/NuTone Div.
Scovill Mfg. Co.
Madison & Red Bank Rds.
Cincinnati, OH 45227

Kohler Co.
Kohler, WI 53044

Powers-Fiat
Div. Powers Regulator Co.
3400 Oakton
Skokie, IL 60076

Universal-Rundle Corp.
217 N. Mill St.
New Castle, PA 16103

Williams Div.
Leigh Products, Inc.
1536 Grant St.
Elkhart, IN 46514

Floorcovering

American Olean Tile Co.
1000 Cannon Ave.
Lansdale, PA 19446

Amsterdam Corp.
950 Third Ave.
New York, NY 10022

Armstrong Cork Co.
W. Liberty & Charlotte
Lancaster, PA 17604

Azrock Floor Products
Box 531
500 Main Plaza Bldg.
San Antonio, TX 78292

Bangkok Industries, Inc.
1900 S. 20th St.
Philadelphia, PA 19145

Bigelow-Sanford
Box 3089
Greenville, SC 29602

Bruce Hardwood Floors
A Triangle Pacific Co.
P. O. Box 171802
Memphis, TN 38117

Burlington House Carpets
Valley Forge Corp. Center
King of Prussia, PA 19406

Congoleum Corp.
195 Belgrove Dr.
Kearny, NJ 07032

Ege Rya
919 Third Ave.
New York, NY 10022

Florida Tile Industries, Inc.
Lakeland, FL 33801

GAF Corp.
140 W. 51st St.
New York, NY 10020

Interpace Corp.
2901 Los Feliz Blvd.
Los Angeles, CA 90039

Kentile Floors, Inc.
58 2nd Ave.
Brooklyn, NY 11215

National Floor
Products Co., Inc.
P. O. Box 354
Florence, AL 35630

Tile Council of America
P. O. Box 503
Mahwah, NJ 07430

U. S. Ceramic Tile Co.
1375 Raff Rd., S. W.
Canton, OH 44710

Wood Mosaic
Box 21159
Louisville, KY 40221

Furniture

American Drew, Inc.
Box 489
No. Wilkesboro, NC 28659

Bassett Furniture Industries
Bassett, VA 24055

Bedlam Brass Beds
19-21 Fair Lawn Ave.
Fair Lawn, NJ 07410

Bernhardt Industries, Inc.
1540 Morganton Blvd., SW
Lenoir, NC 28645

Brazil Industries Corp.
4 East 34th St.
New York, NY 10016

Broyhill Furniture
Box 700
Lenoir, NC 28633

Butcher Block Warehouse
320 Terry Ave.
Seattle, WA 98109

Cado
Royal System
58-08 39th Ave.
Woodside, NY 11377

Calif-Asia Div.
Brown Jordan
Box 1269
El Monte, CA 91734

Chromcraft Furniture
1 Quality Ln.
Senatobia, MS 38668

Cosco Home Products
2525 State St.
Columbus, IN 47201

James David
128 Weldon Pkwy
Maryland Hts, MO 63043

Davis Cabinet Co.
Box 60444
Nashville, TN 37206

DeSoto
Box 492
Jackson, MS 39205

Directional Industries
979 Third Ave.
New York, NY 10022

Ello Furniture Mfg. Co.
1034 Elm St.
Rockford, IL 61101

Founders Furniture
P. O. Box 339
Thomasville, NC 27360

Hickory Mfg. Co.
Hickory, NC 28601

Howard Family Room
Furnishings
Box 732
Starksville, MS 39759

Kroehler Mfg. Co.
222 E. 5th St.
Naperville, IL 60540

Landes Mfg. Co.
14201 S. Main St.
Los Angeles, CA 90061

The Lane Co.
Altavista, VA 24517

Peters-Revington
100 N. Washington St.
Delphi, IN 46923

Pipe Dream Mfg.
1524 S. Dixie Hwy.
Pompano Beach, FL 33060

Schoolfield Furniture Ind.
Mullins, SC 29574

Selig Mfg. Co.
Leominster, MA 01453

Simmons Co.
2 Park Ave.
New York, NY 10016

Spherical Furniture Co.
Boone, NC 28607

Stanley Furniture Co.
Stanleytown, VA 24168

Stratford Co.
932 American Mart
666 Lakeshore Dr.
Chicago, IL 60611

Syroco
Syracuse, NY 13201

Thomasville Furniture
Inds., Inc.
P. O. Box 339
Thomasville, NC 27360

Kitchen Cabinets

Connor Forest Industries
Box 847
Wausau, WI 54401

Coppes, Inc.
455 E. Market St.
Nappanee, IN 46550

Excel Wood Products Co.
Box 819
Lakewood, NJ 08701

Haas Cabinet Co.
Sellersburg, IN 47172

International Paper Co.
Long-Bell Cabinet Div.
Box 8411
Portland, OR 97207

IXL Div.
Westinghouse Electric Corp.
R. R. 1
Elizabeth City, NC 27909

Merillat Industries, Inc.
2075 W. Beecher Rd.
Adrian, MI 49221

Mutschler Bros. Co.
South Madison St.
Nappanee, IN 46550

Poggenpohl/USA
222 Cedar Lane
Teaneck, NJ 07666

Quaker Maid Kitchens
Div. Tappan Co.
Leesport, PA 19533

Riviera Products
1960 Seneca Rd.
St. Paul, MN 35122

H. J. Scheirich Co.
Box 21037
Louisville, KY 40221

St. Charles Mfg. Co.
551 Tyler Rd.
St. Charles, IL 60174

Triangle Pacific Cabinet Corp.
4255 LBJ Freeway
Dallas, TX 75234

United Cabinet Corp.
Box 420
Jasper, IN 47546

Wood-Mode Cabinetry
Snyder County
Kreamer, PA 17833

Walls & Windows

Abitibi Corp.
3250 W. Big Beaver Rd.
Troy, MI 48084

American Plywood Assn.
1119 A St.
Tacoma, WA 98401

Andersen Corp.
Bayport, MN 55003

Biltbest Corp.
175 Coyne St.
Ste. Genevieve, MO 63670

California Redwood Assn.
617 Montgomery St.
San Francisco, CA 94111

Caradco Div.
Scovill Mfg. Co.
1098 Jackson St.
Dubuque, IA 52001

Clopay Corp.
Clopay Sq.
Cincinnati, OH 45214

Dacor, Inc.
65 Armory St.
Worcester, MA 01601

Jack Denst Designs, Inc.
7355 S. Exchange Ave.
Chicago, IL 60649

E. I. DuPont De Nemours
& Co.
Wilmington, DE 19898

General Tire & Rubber Co.
1 General St.
Akron, OH 44309

Georgia-Pacific Corp.
900 S. W. 5th Ave.
Portland, OR 97204

Graber Co.
Graber Plaza
Middleton, WI 53562

W. R. Grace & Co.
Wallcovering Div.
1255 Lynnfield Rd.
Memphis, TN 38138

Imperial Wallpaper Mill, Inc.
23645 Mercantile Rd.
Cleveland, OH 44122

Joanna Western Mills
2141 S. Jefferson St.
Chicago, IL 60616

Kenney Mfg. Co.
Warwick, RI 02887

Levolor Lorentzen, Inc.
720 Monroe St.
Hoboken, NJ 07030

LouverDrape, Inc.
1100 Colorado Ave.
Santa Monica, CA 90400

Marvin Windows
Warroad, MN 56763

Masonite Corp.
29 N. Wacker Dr.
Chicago, IL 60606

Red Cedar Shingle & Handsplit
Shake Bureau
515 116th Ave. NE
Bellevue, WA 98004

Rolscreen Co.
100 Main St.
Pella, IA 50219

James Seeman Studios, Inc.
50 Rose Pl.
Garden City Park, NY 11530

United-DeSoto
3101 S. Kedzie Ave.
Chicago, IL 60623

U. S. Plywood Div.
Champion International
1 Landmark Sq.
Stamford, CT 06921

Wallcovering Industry Bureau
1099 Wall St. West
Lyndhurst, NJ 07071

Weyerhaeuser Co.
P. O. Box 1188
Chesapeake, VA 23320

Window Shade Mfrs. Assn.
230 Park Ave.
New York, NY 10017

Exciting home planning ideas

Ideas for every facet of home planning, home plans in every architectural style that you can buy and build, as well as a complete guide to your home product needs and a practical solution to the mysteries of solar energy systems are yours direct from the Bantam/Hudson Planning Center.

See order form below.

Bantam/Hudson Plans Books

An outstanding collection of home plans to buy, in every architectural style. Designs for every section of the country at a price you can afford. Also Home Improvement Projects. Each $2.95.

100 Custom Home Plans 112 pages
Colonial Home Plans 112 pages
Contemporary Home Plans 112 pages
Small Home Plans 112 pages
Leisure Home Plans 112 pages
Home Improvement Project Ideas
80 pages

200 Most Popular Home Plans

The most diverse collection of popular style home plans in print. 200 pre-designed plans for year-round and vacation homes, plus some newly developed solar home plans. Working drawings available for each plan. 256 pages. $2.25.

Bantam/Hudson Idea Books

A picture-packed series of elegant home planning ideas for your new home, your vacation home or that long-planned remodeling project designed to make your home a better place to live. Each $4.95.

Kitchen Ideas 112 pages
Bathroom Ideas 112 pages
Decks and Patios 112 pages
Fireplace Ideas 112 pages
Remodeling Ideas 128 pages
Bonus Rooms 128 pages
Bedroom Ideas 128 pages
Vacation Homes 128 pages

A Practical Guide to Solar Homes

All the basic information you need if you are thinking solar. Includes thirty solar and energy-conserving home plans to buy and a comprehensive listing of products on the market. 144 pages. $6.95.

Please send me the books I have checked

☐ Bathroom Ideas M1022 $4.95
☐ Bedroom Ideas 01044-1 $4.95
☐ Bonus Rooms 01045-X $4.95
☐ Decks & Patios M1023 $4.95
☐ Fireplace Ideas M1025 $4.95
☐ Kitchen Ideas M1024 $4.95
☐ Remodeling Ideas 01047-6 $4.95
☐ Vacation Homes 01046-8 $4.95
☐ 100 Custom Homes M1019 $2.95
☐ Colonial Home Plans 01075-1 $2.95
☐ Contemporary Home Plans 01076-X $2.95
☐ Small Home Plans M01133-2 $2.95
☐ Leisure Home Plans M01134-0 $2.95

☐ Home Improvement Project Ideas M1018 $2.95
☐ Practical Guide to Solar Homes
M01132-4 $6.95
☐ 200 Most Popular Home Plans B11758-0 $2.25

(Include 50¢ for each of the above books for postage and handling)

☐ All 16 Books $55.90 postage paid
The books listed here would cost $74.50 if ordered separately. You can have the whole set of 16 books for just $55.90 and we will pay postage — this saves you $18.60!

☐ Master Charge
☐ Visa/BankAmericard

Card # _____

Payment enclosed $ _____

Exp. date _____

Name _____

Address _____

City _____ State _____ Zip _____

Make check or Money Order payable to Hudson Home Guides

Bantam/Hudson Books 289 South San Antonio Road, Los Altos, California 94022

How To Order Your Home Plans

- Enter plan number and number of sets wanted on order form as indicated.

- Mirror reverse plans have all lettering and dimensions reading backwards. If ordering mirror reverse, you will need at least one set of regular plans.

- Materials list and reverse plans are available only when noted in plans copy.

- Specify on order form if you want materials list or reverse plans.

- If you plan to build, we suggest a minimum of 6-8 sets for your lender, builder, subcontractors, local building departments, etc.

- PLANS HOTLINE — For Master Charge or Visa cardholders only. You may speed your plans order by dialing TOLL FREE 800-227-8393. (California residents phone direct 415-941-6700.)

Plan Prices

1 set $75; 4 sets $105; 8 sets $148; each additional set $12

Plan	Page	Plan	Page	Plan	Page	Plan	Page	Plan	Page	Plan	Page
2061	98	2649	81	3421	64	3858	74	4214	73	6206	13
2062	41	2746	48	3422	102	3860	65	4215	20	6407	78
2064	68	2747	21	3622	43	3862	45	4216	49	6702	75
2130	101	2748	95	3630	46	3869	100	4345	22	6703	106
2152	25	2749	77	3631	93	3917	51	4346	18	6803	70
2263	10	3222	36	3632	67	3941	97	5004	27	6804	52
2264	15	3223	40	3801	19	3949	71	5105	11	7207	23
2347	80	3224	53	3802	24	4048	76	5205	104	7208	37
2348	94	3225	42	3813	79	4049	99	5302	17	7504	47
2425	96	3328	44	3816	92	4050	103	6013	14	7505	66
2519	16	3337	72	3838	39	4110	107	6014	26		
2648	69	3401	50	3844	105	4213	12	6015	38		

Mail to: **HOME PLANS**
Hudson Home Publications
289 S. San Antonio Road
Los Altos, Calif. 94022

Order Form

Please send me _____ sets of
blueprints for Plan No. _____ Cost: $ _____
Postage and Handling .... $ __2.50__
Allow 10 working days for delivery
California Residents add 6% Sales Tax .... $ _____
TOTAL $ _____

I hereby authorize Hudson Publishing Company to execute a sales slip on my behalf against my
☐ Master Charge   ☐ Visa

master charge · THE INTERBANK CARD   VISA®

Card Exp. _____

Your Signature _____

Name (print) _____

Address _____

City _____ State _____ Zip _____

Phone (_____) - _____ - _____

Make Check or Money Order Payable to Hudson Home Publications /H

(Sorry, no C.O.D.'s)

Mail to: **HOME PLANS**
Hudson Home Publications
289 S. San Antonio Road
Los Altos, Calif. 94022

Order Form

Please send me _____ sets of
blueprints for Plan No. _____ Cost: $ _____
Postage and Handling .... $ __2.50__
Allow 10 working days for delivery
California Residents add 6% Sales Tax .... $ _____
TOTAL $ _____

I hereby authorize Hudson Publishing Company to execute a sales slip on my behalf against my
☐ Master Charge   ☐ Visa

master charge · THE INTERBANK CARD   VISA®

Card Exp. _____

Your Signature _____

Name (print) _____

Address _____

City _____ State _____ Zip _____

Phone (_____) - _____ - _____

Make Check or Money Order Payable to Hudson Home Publications /H

(Sorry, no C.O.D.'s)